D0845786

Trade and Wages

Trade and Wages

Leveling Wages Down?

Edited by Jagdish Bhagwati
and
Marvin H. Kosters

The AEI Press

Publisher for the American Enterprise Institute
WASHINGTON, D.C.

1994

*The American Enterprise Institute acknowledges with gratitude the support
of the General Electric Foundation, Inc., for the publication of this volume.*

Library of Congress Cataloging-in-Publication Data

Trade and wages / edited by Jagdish Bhagwati and Marvin H. Kosters.
   p. cm.
   Essays from a one-day workshop on the influence of trade on jobs
and wages, American Enterprise Institute, September 10, 1993.
   Includes bibliographical references.
   ISBN 0-8447-3858-1 (c). ISBN 0-8447-3859-X (pbk.)
   1. Wages. 2. Labor market. 3. Free trade. I. Bhagwati, Jagdish
N., 1934- . II. Kosters, Marvin H. III. American Enterprise
Institute for Public Policy Research.
  HD4906.T7 1994
  331.2′1—dc20   94-13297
                                            CIP

THE AEI PRESS
Publisher for the American Enterprise Institute
1150 17th Street, N.W., Washington, D.C. 20036

Printed in the United States of America

Contents

LIST OF TABLES

Contributors

JAGDISH BHAGWATI is Arthur Lehman Professor of Economics and professor of political science at Columbia University. He is also a visiting scholar at the American Enterprise Institute. Professor Bhagwati's contributions in international trade theory are recognized around the world, and he has recently served as economic policy adviser to the director-general of GATT. One of his best-known recent books is *Protectionism*.

MARVIN H. KOSTERS is resident scholar and director of economic policy studies at the American Enterprise Institute. He has written extensively on labor market developments, including recent trends in wage patterns and the distribution of income. He recently edited *Workers and Their Wages: Changing Patterns in the United States*.

ALAN V. DEARDORFF is professor of economics and public policy and chair of the Department of Economics at the University of Michigan. In addition to his work on the theory of comparative advantage and on trade policy issues, he has developed influential empirical models to explain the patterns and effects of trade. Professor Deardorff is coauthor of *Computational Analysis of Global Trading Arrangements*.

VIVEK H. DEHEJIA is a graduate student and Ph.D. candidate at Columbia University.

DALIA S. HAKURA is a graduate student and Ph.D. candidate at the University of Michigan.

Preface

The essays in this volume were presented at a workshop on the influence of trade on jobs and wages at the American Enterprise Institute, September 10, 1993.

The impact of freer trade on the real wages of the unskilled has become a sufficiently important issue in the political domain for the economic arguments and evidence on the subject to be examined in depth from a scholarly point of view. The central role the issue played in the NAFTA debate, with Ross Perot and Pat Choate aligned with the labor unions on an excessively pessimistic assessment of the outcome, has confirmed this importance.

The first chapter, by Marvin Kosters, sets out the salient empirical evidence on the question of real wages of the unskilled and the wage differential between the skilled and the unskilled. The central findings of relevance are:

- The average worker's real compensation has increased much less rapidly in the United States since the early 1970s than in the 1950s and 1960s. Japan and the advanced industrial European economies experienced a comparably proportionate slowdown. This stagnation was more pronounced for the wage component of compensation in the United States, and for some demographic groups real wages declined for much of the past twenty years.
- The structure of relative wages in the United States changed markedly during the 1970s and 1980s. Changes that can be characterized as increased returns to human capital investment include a rise in the wage premium for work experience (for college-level workers in the 1970s and for high school–level workers in the 1980s) and a pronounced rise in schooling wage premiums in the 1980s.
- Many broad measures of wage dispersion show substantial increases since the late 1970s. Although these increases represent something of a departure from earlier experience, dispersion within schooling and experience groups was increasing throughout the 1970s.
- An increase in wage dispersion and a corresponding rise in the

price of skills took place in several advanced industrial countries. The United States and the United Kingdom experienced increases that were much larger than in other countries, some of which experienced little or no change. Other labor market indicators suggest, however, that institutional and regulatory constraints muted the effect on wage structures in these latter countries.

The second chapter, by Jagdish Bhagwati and Vivek Dehejia, and the third chapter, by Alan Deardorff and Dalia Hakura, address directly the question of the relationship between trade and wages. On the one hand, Bhagwati and Dehejia concentrate on the key question: does the freeing of trade hurt the real wages of the unskilled? On the other hand, Deardorff and Hakura properly distinguish among several different questions that could be raised. For instance, if technical change occurs in the economy and tends to drive down the real wages of the unskilled, does the presence of free trade moderate or accentuate the adverse effect on those real wages? The different possible questions that Deardorff and Hakura consider are used to explore the interpretation that can be placed on results from empirical studies on trade and wages. Their questions and their comprehensive evaluations of several recent studies provide a useful compass for analysts to study the connections between trade and real wage patterns.

The central policy-related question, however, remains that posed and addressed by Bhagwati and Dehejia. Their analysis of the theoretical arguments stems from the factor price equalization and Stopler-Samuelson theorems, and it is generally understood to imply that freer trade with poor countries necessarily reduces the real wages of our unskilled labor. This analysis shows excellent and compelling reasons why that inference is too hasty. The assumptions that lead to the theorems and the feared outcomes on real wages of the unskilled are not realistic. Once they are abandoned, the real wages of the unskilled can be shown to rise when free trade with the unskilled-abundant poor countries is analyzed. Indeed, a recently computed model of U.S.-Mexico trade by Brown, Deardorff, and Stern, which builds into itself some of these changed assumptions (especially increasing returns in production), shows precisely that NAFTA could *increase* the real wages of the unskilled in the United States.

The Bhagwati-Dehejia essay also rejects, on such conceptual grounds, oft-cited and key empirical studies claiming to show that trade has hurt real wages in the 1980s. The empirical evidence does not show the relative prices of imported, unskilled-laborer-intensive industries to have fallen; in fact, those prices have risen. The contention that the factor prices changed as they did in the 1980s because of trade—when in fact goods prices changed in a way opposite to what would happen if trade were the explanatory factor—is illogical and hence unpersuasive.

Nonetheless, Bhagwati and Dehejia explore alternative ways in which, regardless of goods-price behavior, changing trade might have been a source of declining real wages. In particular, they argue that increasing randomization of comparative advantage in manufactures because of globalization may imply higher labor turnover. This in turn could reduce skill-acquisition on the job by the unskilled, and hence reduce improvement in their real wages over time.

This volume thus offers strong skepticism concerning the evidence in support of the fear that freer trade has been pushing down the wages of the unskilled, or that it will do so in the future. It also offers new ideas for further exploration, both theoretical and empirical, on the subject. As such, it should be of value both to policy-making economists and to scholars of international trade and labor.

Trade and Wages

1
An Overview of Changing Wage Patterns in the Labor Market

Marvin H. Kosters

Among the important changes taking place in the labor market in the 1980s, one of the most prominent was a pronounced increase in the relative wages of skilled workers. This change in the structure of relative wages resulted in lower real wage levels for some less skilled workers, because it came at a time of real wage stagnation for the average worker. A growing number of research efforts emerged to measure and document the kinds of labor market changes that occurred and to examine evidence on their possible causes.[1]

This chapter describes the main results of this research and discusses some of the proposed explanations. The purpose of this overview is to describe the patterns of change in wages to provide background for analysis of whether they might be traced in part to international trade sources.

The discussion begins with a list of the most important features of recent wage trends and changing wage patterns. Trends in average wages and employment are then described briefly. Changes in relative wage patterns in the United States that have been documented in research studies are then described in more detail. The main focus is on wage developments in the U.S. labor market, but information is

---

1. Much of this research is summarized in a major review article in the *Journal of Economic Literature* by Frank Levy and Richard Murnane (1992). Several relevant studies are available in books edited by Burtless (1990) and by Kosters (1991), and others were published in the February 1992 issue of the *Quarterly Journal of Economics*. In addition, the *Employment Outlook* (1993) published by the OECD draws on many of these studies, on a series of important studies by scholars affiliated with the National Bureau of Economic Research, and on various other studies. Many relevant references are cited in these studies and reviews. The list of references following this chapter is far from exhaustive, because valuable and relevant studies that are available are too numerous to list or review in detail in this brief overview.

also presented on changes in other industrial countries. Finally, research on possible sources of some of the changes in relative wage patterns is discussed.

Major Changes in Wage Patterns

The following changes in wage patterns seem most important for characterizing recent changes in the labor market:

• A slowdown in productivity growth in the U.S. economy since the early 1970s is generally recognized. The more sluggish behavior of real hourly compensation implied by this slowdown was widely shared among other advanced industrial countries, but these other countries generally experienced growth in pay that was stronger and employment that was weaker than in the United States.

• Wage dispersion increased markedly from the late 1970s to the late 1980s. If wages are regarded at least approximately as measures of values of marginal products of workers, and if we identify levels of workers' value of marginal products with skill levels, this increase in the dispersion of wages is equivalent to a rise in skill premiums or an increase in economic returns to skills.

• Rising wage dispersion in the 1980s was marked by a strong rise in wage premiums for additional years of schooling. The widening of wage differentials by years of schooling extends across the entire range of schooling levels, although it is most often illustrated and described in terms of the college–high school wage premium. After declining during most of the 1970s, the college–high school wage premium increased during the 1980s to a level higher than in any earlier year for which comparable data are available.

• The economic return to increased work experience, an alternative way of acquiring human capital, also rose. The return to work experience for college-level workers increased substantially since the early 1970s, but a more pronounced increase in returns to work experience for high school–level workers took place mainly in the 1980s.

• The deterioration in the relative wages of workers with low schooling and little work experience in the 1980s resulted in a decline in real wage levels for many workers defined in terms of fixed, low levels of schooling and work experience.

• Even though the wage premium for years of schooling declined gradually during much of the 1970s before it reversed and increased sharply during the 1980s, evidence suggests that the wage premium for higher skills (higher earning capabilities) began increasing much

2

earlier. Wage dispersion within age, schooling, and other categories was increasing throughout the 1970s and 1980s.

• Wage differences by gender declined; women's wages rose substantially, relative to men's, during the 1980s.

• The gradual convergence of wages of black workers toward levels of white workers was interrupted in the late 1970s. Relative wages for black workers stagnated, apparently in large part because their schooling and skill levels were lower than for the average worker. Wages for black workers were therefore more likely to decline with increasing wage dispersion.

• The increase in wage dispersion in the late 1970s and 1980s followed a period of considerable stability in wage patterns during most of the postwar period. This relative stability followed a decline in wage dispersion that took place during the 1940s, perhaps in connection with the production patterns and price and allocation controls of the wartime economy.

• The increase in wage dispersion in the 1980s was larger in the United States than in other advanced industrial countries. The United Kingdom also experienced fairly large increases. Several countries experienced small increases, however, and countries that experienced little or no increase in measured dispersion seem to have been subject to labor market conditions that might have produced increased wage dispersion if wage adjustments had not been blunted by institutional or regulatory constraints.

Wages and Employment

A brief overview of trends in average wages and employment is useful before turning to changes in relative wages and dispersion. The data on real hourly compensation charted in figure 1–1 show both the slowdown in growth of average real hourly compensation and the convergence of compensation in other industrial countries toward U.S. levels. These measures of compensation per hour cover only production workers in manufacturing except for the United States, where compensation for the total private nonfarm sector is shown separately in addition. These hourly compensation measures are charted in logarithmic form to highlight the slowdown in growth that they all share. For most of these countries, the slowdown in growth rate and in convergence toward U.S. levels began in the early 1970s.

Comparisons of employment growth since 1973 are shown in figure 1–2. The most striking feature of this figure is the amount of employment growth in North America compared with that in the

3

FIGURE 1–1
REAL HOURLY COMPENSATION OF MANUFACTURING PRODUCTION WORKERS IN TEN INDUSTRIAL COUNTRIES, 1960–1992

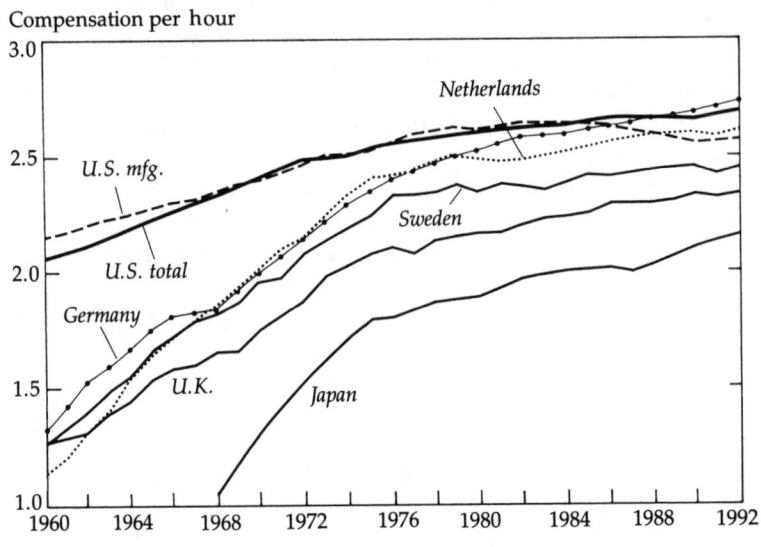

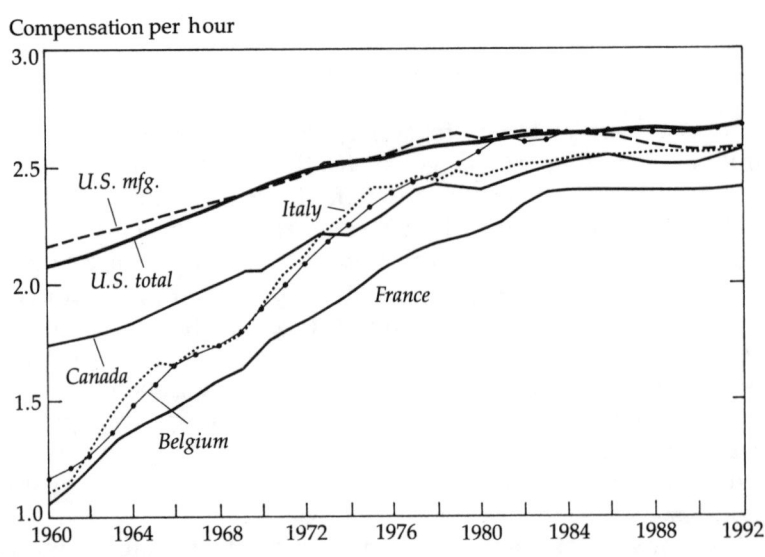

NOTE: In natural logarithms of 1987 U.S. dollars, deflated by purchasing power parity price indexes.
SOURCE: Bureau of Labor Statistics.

FIGURE 1–2
CUMULATIVE EMPLOYMENT GROWTH IN THE PUBLIC AND PRIVATE SECTORS IN
NORTH AMERICA, THE EUROPEAN COMMUNITY, AND JAPAN, 1973–1991
(change in thousands)

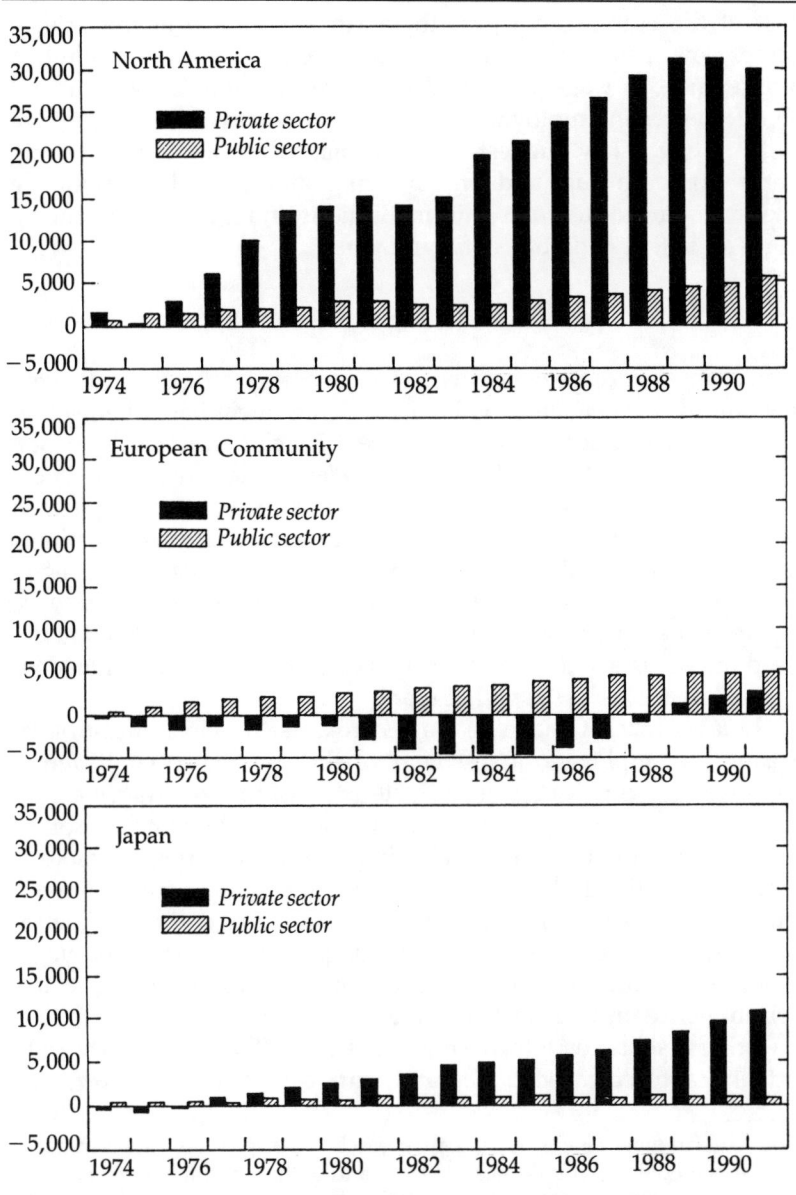

SOURCE: Organization for Economic Cooperation and Development.

5

European Community. It provides a graphic illustration of the "job creation miracle" in the United States, as seen from Europe. A second noteworthy feature is the preponderant share of private-sector job growth in North America, compared with public-sector job growth that outstripped private-sector growth in the European Community. Most of the employment growth in Japan was also in the private sector. How these differences in employment growth may be linked to differences in wage levels and structures is not entirely clear, but the differences in employment patterns are so striking that they are worth noting. They suggest the possibility that differences among countries in both wage and employment patterns may be attributable at least in part to differences in institutions and policies influencing wages and other conditions of employment.

The Increase in Wage Dispersion

Small changes in dispersion in wages or incomes have usually attracted only limited research attention because such changes have often subsequently been reversed. When a persistent increase in wage dispersion became apparent during the 1980s, evidence that wage differences between workers with different schooling levels were widening helped explain why. The timing of the increase in schooling wage premiums suggested that a significant change in wage behavior might have begun in the 1980s or slightly earlier. Some research showed that wage dispersion began rising several years earlier, however. This finding raised questions about whether wage behavior in the 1980s should be regarded as a sharp break with the past.

In labor market analyses, wages are a useful, albeit incomplete, measure of employers' assessment of the productive contribution that a worker with particular characteristics can make. Wages are an incomplete measure, of course, because nonwage benefits and other conditions of employment are also important. Measures of workers' characteristics that indicate their value to an employer are even more limited. To measure skills in labor market research, primary reliance is usually placed on years of school completed and estimated years of work experience, because these measures are widely available and their influence on wages has been demonstrated.[2] Other dimensions of workers' skills for which employers are willing to pay are only partially captured by schooling and work experience, however, and

---

2. This framework for empirical research on wages and labor markets was pioneered by Jacob Mincer (1974), and it has become the standard approach to analysis of earning capabilities.

some may not be reflected at all. Consequently, wage variation that remains after schooling and work experience are taken into account can be attributed in part to dimensions of skill that are not easily measured but nonetheless perceptible to employers.

A useful study by Chinhui Juhn, Kevin M. Murphy, and Brooks Pierce (1993) builds on these concepts to describe and interpret the rise in wage inequality.[3] They examine trends in the distribution of real weekly wages of male workers from 1964 to 1988. The remarkable increase in wage dispersion they report is graphically displayed in figure 1–3. It shows that over this twenty-four–year period, the size of wage increases was systematically and almost linearly related to wage levels in the distribution as a whole. Wages at the top of the distribution were nearly 40 percent higher at the end of the period than at the beginning, and real wages declined about 5 percent for those near the bottom.

To examine the timing of the increase in wage dispersion, they compare wage increases across the entire distribution in four subperiods. In figure 1–4, they chart wage increases at each percentile of the distribution relative to the average increase in wages across the distribution as a whole during each subperiod. Only small changes in relative wages occurred during the last part of the 1960s, as shown in the first panel. After about 1970, however, wages in the lower part of the distribution declined sharply relative to the average for the distribution as a whole. From the mid-1970s to the late 1980s, the size of relative wage changes was closely related to their location in the wage distribution. The increase in wage dispersion was spread relatively evenly across the entire distribution, as shown in the last two panels of the figure. These data suggest that the price of skills began to rise by the end of the 1960s.

The total change in wage dispersion can be apportioned among components associated with changes in the wage premiums for schooling and work experience; changes in the proportions of workers in particular schooling and experience categories; and changes that remain after these measurable portions have been taken into account. Changes in the percentage differential in wages

3. To illustrate changes in the structure of wages, I have drawn primarily on studies based on data that were initially developed by Finis Welch and Kevin M. Murphy. These data from the Current Population Survey include demographic and wage information that is reasonably consistent over time, and they have been analyzed in several important papers by Murphy and Welch and by Murphy with various coauthors.

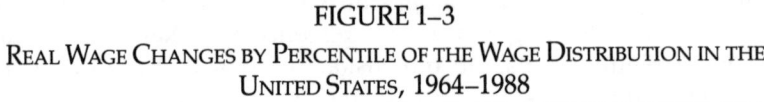

FIGURE 1–3
REAL WAGE CHANGES BY PERCENTILE OF THE WAGE DISTRIBUTION IN THE
UNITED STATES, 1964–1988

Change in log real wage

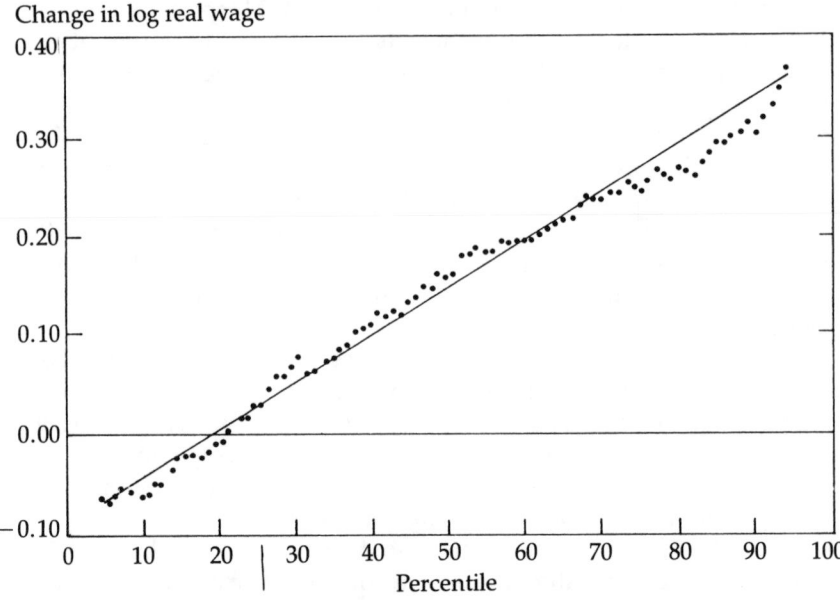

SOURCE: Chinhui Juhn, Kevin M. Murphy, and Brooks Pierce, "Wage Inequality and the Rise in Returns to Skill," *Journal of Political Economy*, June 1993, p. 417.

between the ninetieth and the tenth percentiles of the wage distribution are traced from 1963 to 1989 in figure 1–5, along with the three components into which the total was apportioned. This decomposition shows that changes in the schooling and experience mix have had only small effects on the widening wage spread. It also shows that changes in the wage premiums, or prices, employers are willing to pay for schooling and experience account for a portion that has varied considerably over time, but rose sharply during the 1980s. The last panel of the figure shows that the remaining change in the wage differential, which can be interpreted as the effect of changes in the value of unmeasured skill attributes, has been associated with increased dispersion since 1967. The effect of this component was slightly larger during the 1980s than the combined influence of schooling and work experience. Although wage differentials between schooling levels declined

8

somewhat in the 1970s, the effects on dispersion of this decline were overwhelmed by increases in experience differentials and by increased dispersion within age and schooling categories that were taking place at that time.

The increase in the relative wages of workers with advanced schooling that emerged during the 1980s was a reversal of a small downtrend in the 1970s.[4] The sharp rise in hourly wages for workers with four years of college compared with high school graduates during the 1980s is shown in figure 1–6 from Kevin Murphy and Finis Welch (1993a) for young workers and workers at all experience levels. For new entrants into the work force, the wage premium for college-level workers compared with high school graduates approximately doubled from the late 1970s to the late 1980s. The figure also shows trends in relative wages for recent entrants into the work force (one to five years of potential work experience), compared with those near their peak earning years (twenty-five to thirty-six years of experience). These data cover white males because they constitute the largest component of the work force and because work experience is likely to be more accurately and consistently estimated by potential work experience for males than for females. The general pattern is similar, however, for other demographic groups.

Since skills that are valuable in the workplace are acquired both through work experience and schooling, we might expect a tendency for changes in returns to human capital investment in both forms to move in the same direction. The largest increase in the wage premium for work experience for high school–level workers occurred in the early 1980s, when the schooling-wage premium rose sharply. Both premiums subsided somewhat in the second half of the 1980s. The work-experience premium for high school graduates also rose during the 1970s, however, and the age-earnings profile for college graduates became much steeper during the 1970s, when the college-wage premium was declining. Investments in human capital in these different forms were evidently only partial substitutes in view of these differences in timing. Imperfect substitutability implies that the big changes in relative supplies that occurred during this period may have influenced differences in the timing of wage-premium changes.

Wages of black workers converged toward white workers' wages from the mid-1960s to the mid-1970s. This convergence, more rapid for women than for men, tapered off in the late 1970s. After slumping somewhat during the first part of the 1980s, black relative wages

---

4. The relatively low wage premium for college-level schooling at a time when it also appeared to be declining was described by Freeman (1976).

FIGURE 1–4
CHANGES IN RELATIVE WAGES IN THE UNITED STATES BY PERCENTILE, 1963–1989

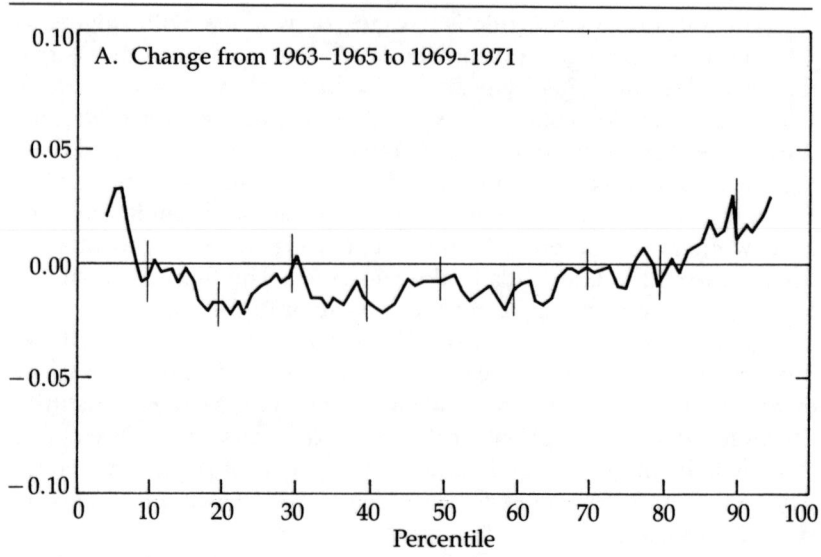

A. Change from 1963–1965 to 1969–1971

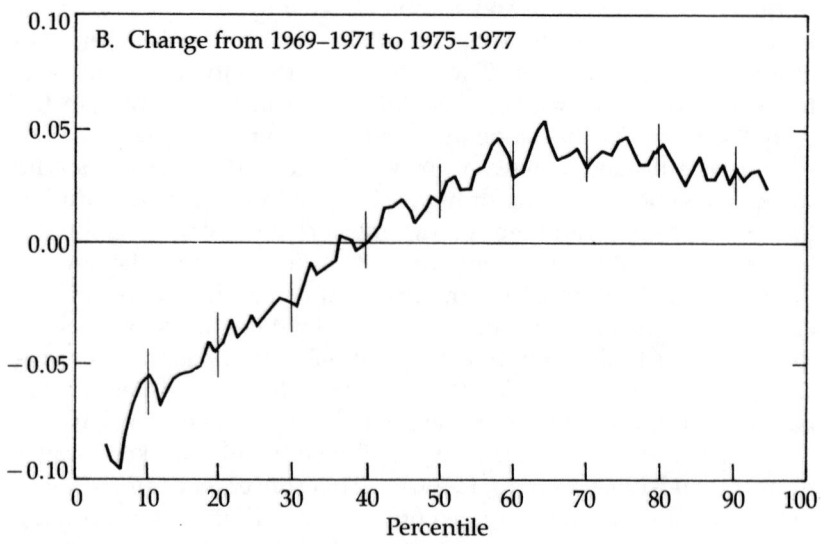

B. Change from 1969–1971 to 1975–1977

FIGURE 1–4 (continued)

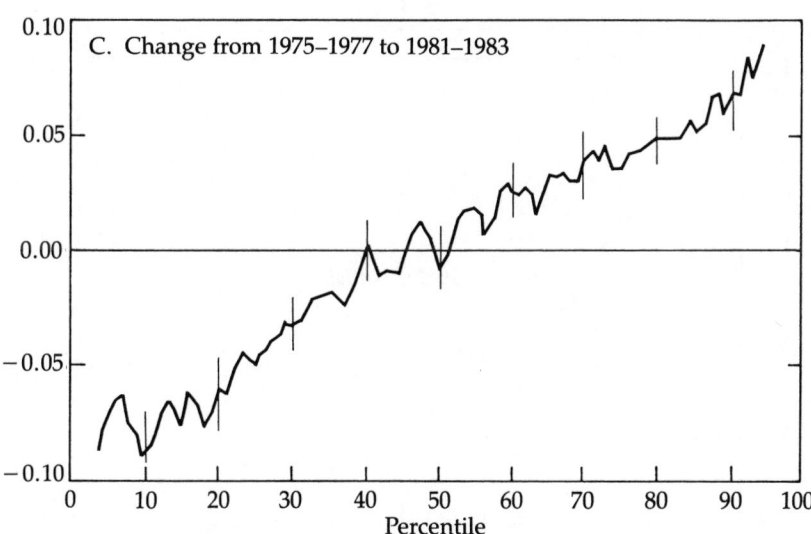

C. Change from 1975–1977 to 1981–1983

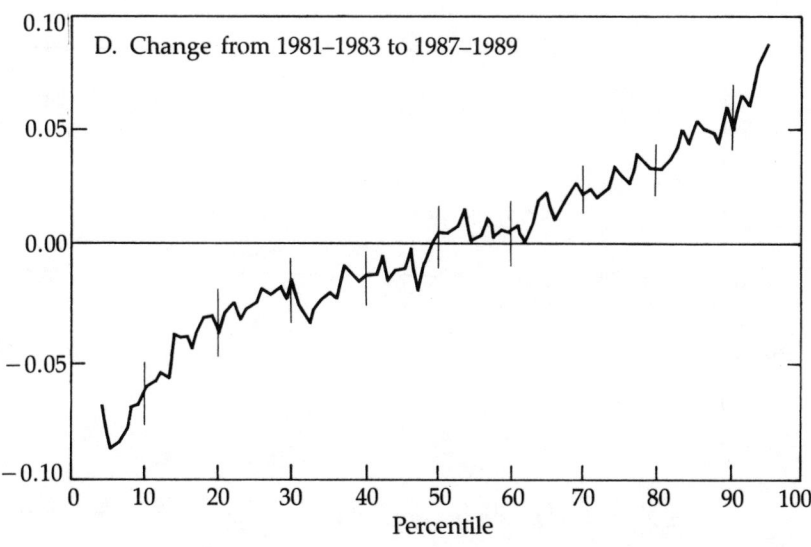

D. Change from 1981–1983 to 1987–1989

NOTE: Units on the vertical axis for each panel are logarithms of relative wages.
SOURCE: Juhn, Murphy, and Pierce, "Wage Inequality," p. 418.

FIGURE 1–5
WAGE DIFFERENTIAL BETWEEN THE NINETIETH AND TENTH PERCENTILES OF THE U.S. WAGE DISTRIBUTION AND COMPONENTS OF THE DIFFERENTIAL, 1963–1989

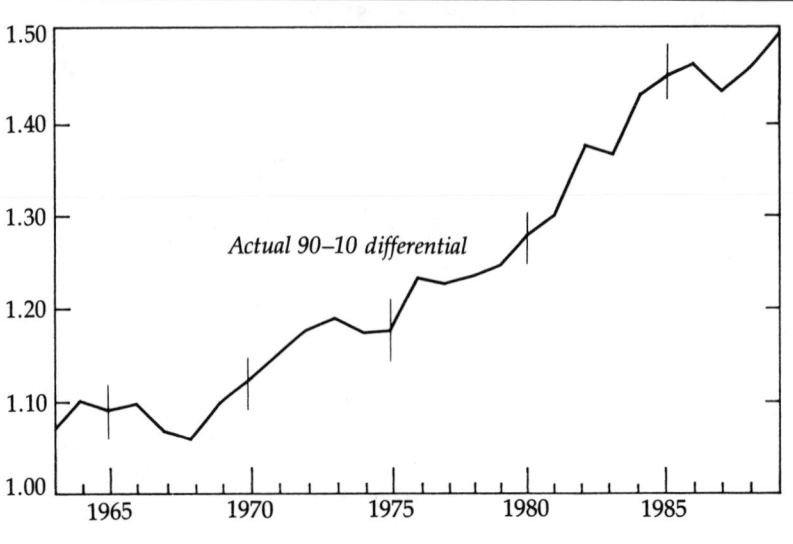

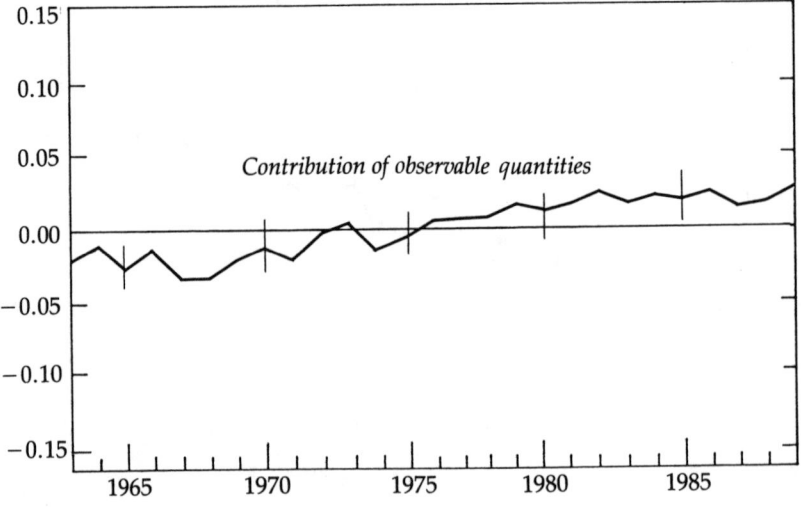

FIGURE 1–5 (continued)

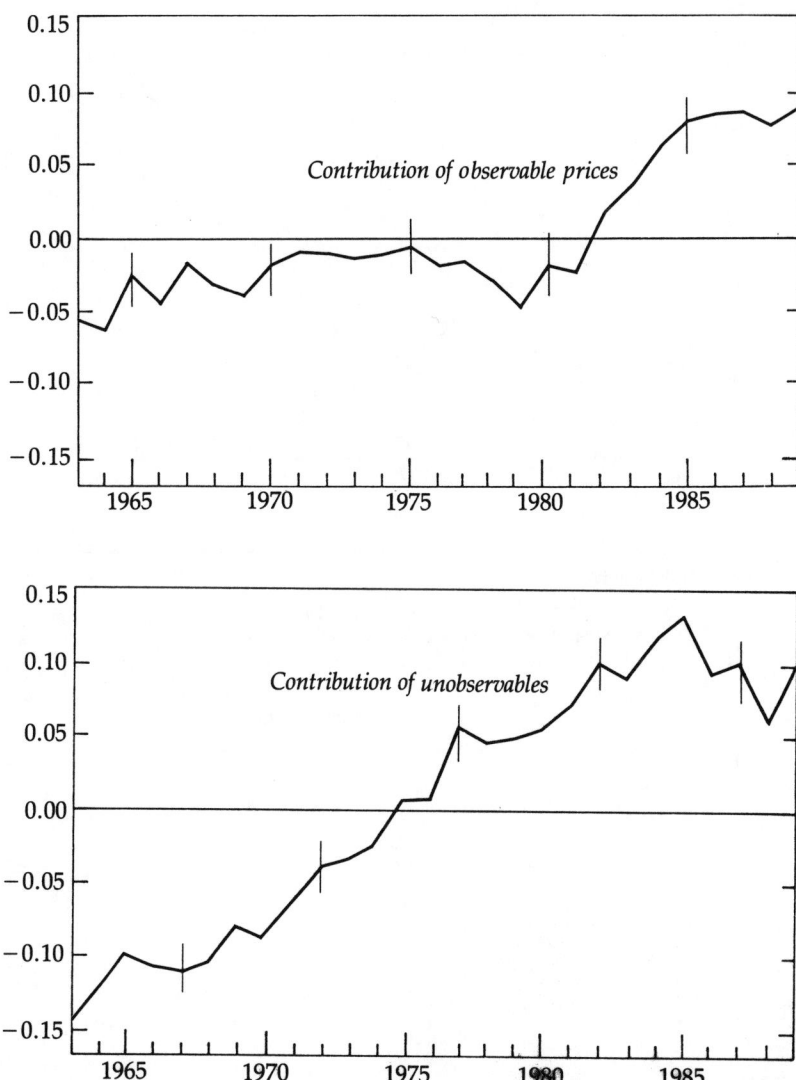

NOTE: Units on the vertical axis for each panel are logarithms of wage differentials.

SOURCE: Juhn, Murphy, and Pierce, "Wage Inequality," p. 427.

FIGURE 1–6
WAGE PREMIUMS FOR EDUCATION AND WORK EXPERIENCE
IN THE UNITED STATES, 1963–1990

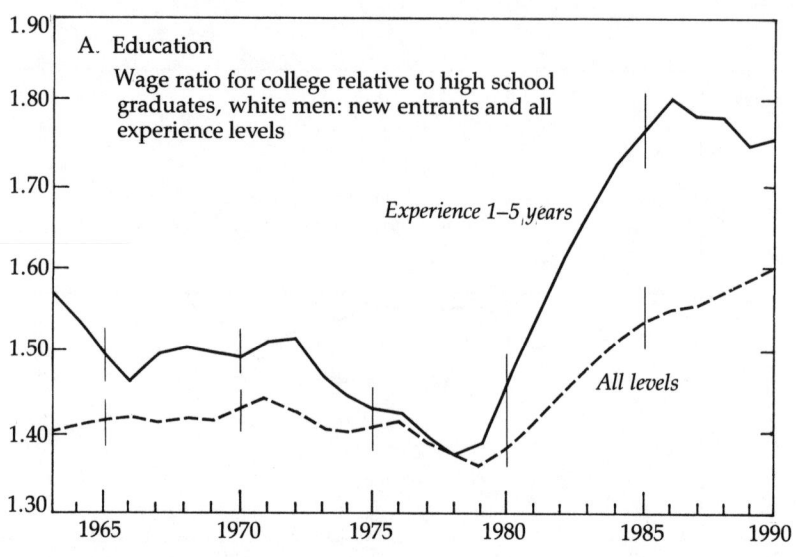

A. Education

Wage ratio for college relative to high school graduates, white men: new entrants and all experience levels

Experience 1–5 years

All levels

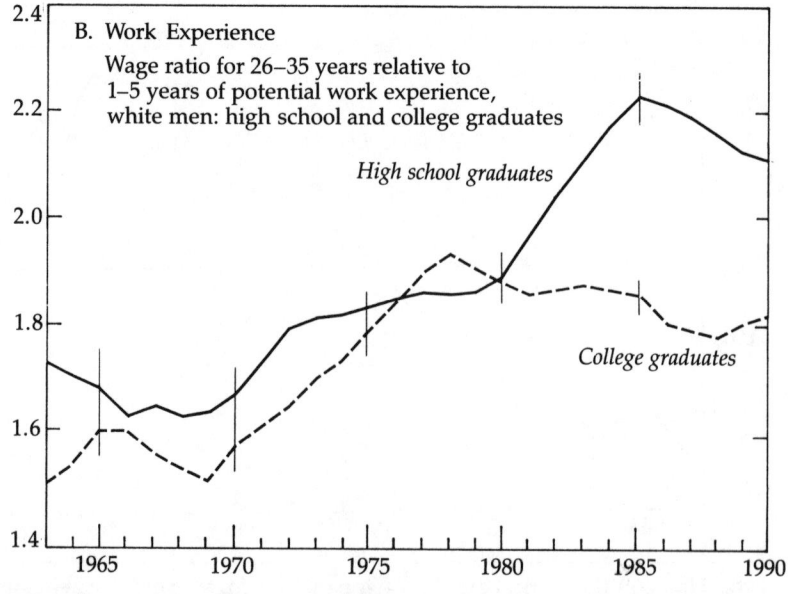

B. Work Experience

Wage ratio for 26–35 years relative to 1–5 years of potential work experience, white men: high school and college graduates

High school graduates

College graduates

SOURCE: Kevin M. Murphy and Finis Welch, *American Economic Review*, May 1993.

began to move up again, as shown in figure 1–7. Despite the slump in their wages relative to white women, black women fared much better than black men in the 1980s because relative wages of white women were moving up sharply, as is also shown in figure 1–7.

In their innovative 1991 analysis, Juhn, Murphy, and Pierce examined wages for black workers by comparing them with wages of white workers at the same level but at a lower position in the white distribution. Their basic insight was that because black workers have lower-than-average schooling levels and wages, black workers fared more poorly than white workers when schooling and skill premiums were increasing. Black wages are much lower, partly because of lower measured skills. Wages of white workers in the lower part of the distribution declined relative to their average. Comparable changes in black and white wage levels would accordingly be associated with poorer average wage performance for black workers than for whites because a larger proportion of them work at wage levels at the lower part of the white wage distribution. These authors attribute almost half the slowdown in wage convergence from 1979 to 1987 to the rise in wage differentials by education and to a slowdown in black-white education convergence.

As has already been noted, women's wages increased relative to men's in the 1980s. The decline in wage differentials by gender was not unique to the United States, as is shown in figure 1–8 from a 1993 study by Francine Blau and Lawrence Kahn. The timing and size of gains in wages of women relative to men varied a good deal among countries. Gains in women's relative wages in the United States compare favorably with those in other countries, but by the end of the 1980s they remained lower than in other countries, with the prominent exception of Japan. Blau and Kahn attribute the larger gender gap in the United States in large part to the wider dispersion in the U.S. wage structure. The gains in relative wages that women achieved in the United States during the 1980s were especially re- markable in the context of widening wage dispersion, which under the method pioneered by Juhn, Murphy, and Pierce (1991) and applied by Blau and Kahn would tend to erode their relative wage po- sition.

An interesting historical feature of wage structure trends in the United States is that wage dispersion narrowed significantly during the 1940s. This change is documented in Claudia Goldin and Robert A. Margo's 1992 study, where they note that the compression may have been attributable to the circumstances of the war years. As they also note, however, the wage structure did not immediately return to its earlier pattern in the postwar years.

FIGURE 1–7
Proportionate Wage Differences by Gender and Race in the United States, 1963–1990

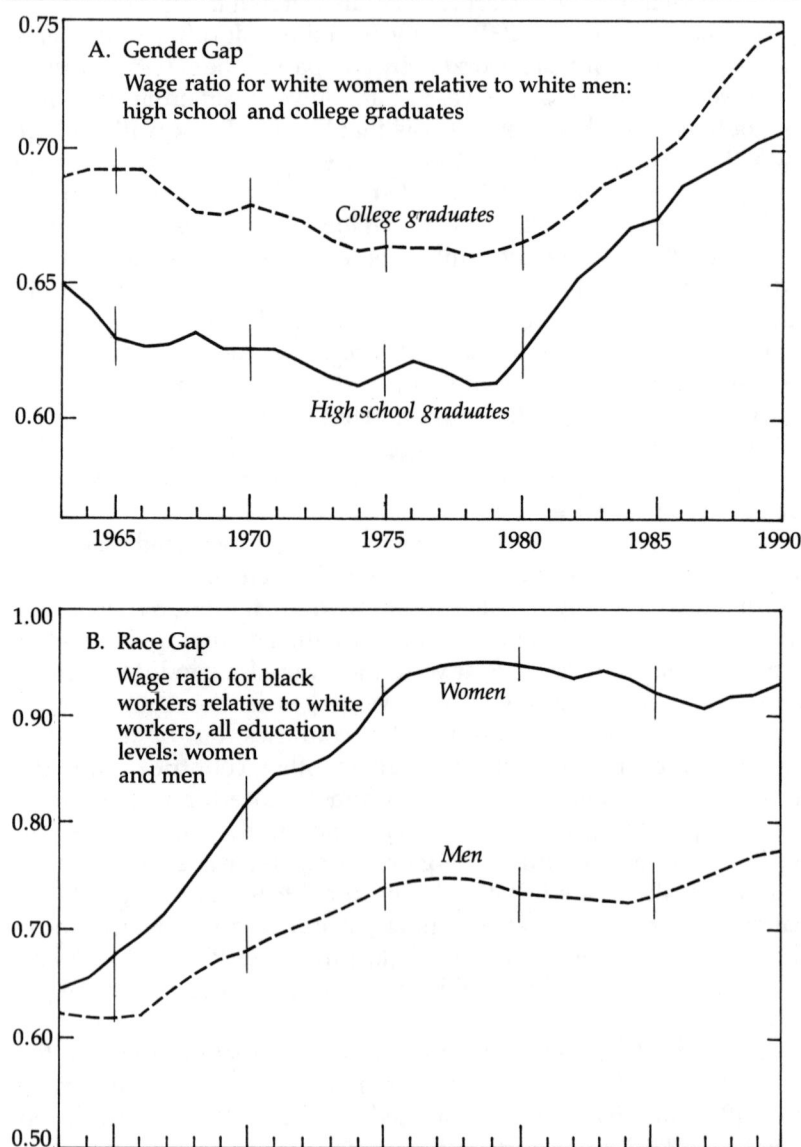

A. Gender Gap
Wage ratio for white women relative to white men: high school and college graduates

College graduates

High school graduates

B. Race Gap
Wage ratio for black workers relative to white workers, all education levels: women and men

Women

Men

Source: Murphy and Welch, *American Economic Review.*

International Comparisons of Wage Trends

Relative wages in several countries have been examined in a number of studies to investigate differences in changes in wage patterns during the past two decades. These studies necessarily rely on data that are not entirely comparable between countries, and the time periods studied depend on data availability. The results of many of these studies have been compared in a recent Organization for Economic Cooperation and Development (OECD) publication that provides a convenient summary of the findings.[5] The discussion here draws mainly on this summary to describe changes in wage patterns for different countries.

Wage dispersion, wages by level of schooling, and wages by workers' age can be compared based on data on wage patterns that are available for several industrial countries. Summary information for comparisons of these three characteristics of wage patterns is reported in table 1–1. These data show that increases in wage dispersion were quite widespread during the 1980s, although not universal. The direction of change in the 1970s and 1980s was toward growing wage differentials for measures of dispersion, for schooling wage premiums, and for age-earnings profiles for most advanced industrial countries for which relevant data are available.

The size and timing of changes differed a great deal among countries as well as among different measures of wage differentials. The United States and the United Kingdom stand out for the size of the increase in dispersion they experienced. Several countries experienced smaller increases in dispersion. In most instances the increases were small enough not to have attracted much attention if they were not part of a broader pattern. In some instances, dispersion only began rising during the 1980s after changes in policy permitted adjustment toward wider wage differentials. In France and the Netherlands, for example, increased dispersion came after retreat from aggressive minimum-wage policies, and in Sweden after retrenchment from its traditional approach to national wage bargaining. In all these countries, with the exception of the United States, rising dispersion in the 1980s followed a period of stable or declining dispersion in the 1970s. The general pattern of a shift toward rising dispersion is fairly clear.

Differences among countries, and especially differences from the United States, may be partly attributable to the way dispersion is measured for these comparisons. In most cases, these measures

---

5. *Employment Outlook*, July 1993, OECD.

FIGURE 1–8

FEMALE-TO-MALE HOURLY EARNINGS RATIOS FOR NONAGRICULTURAL WORKERS IN FIFTEEN COUNTRIES, 1967–1990

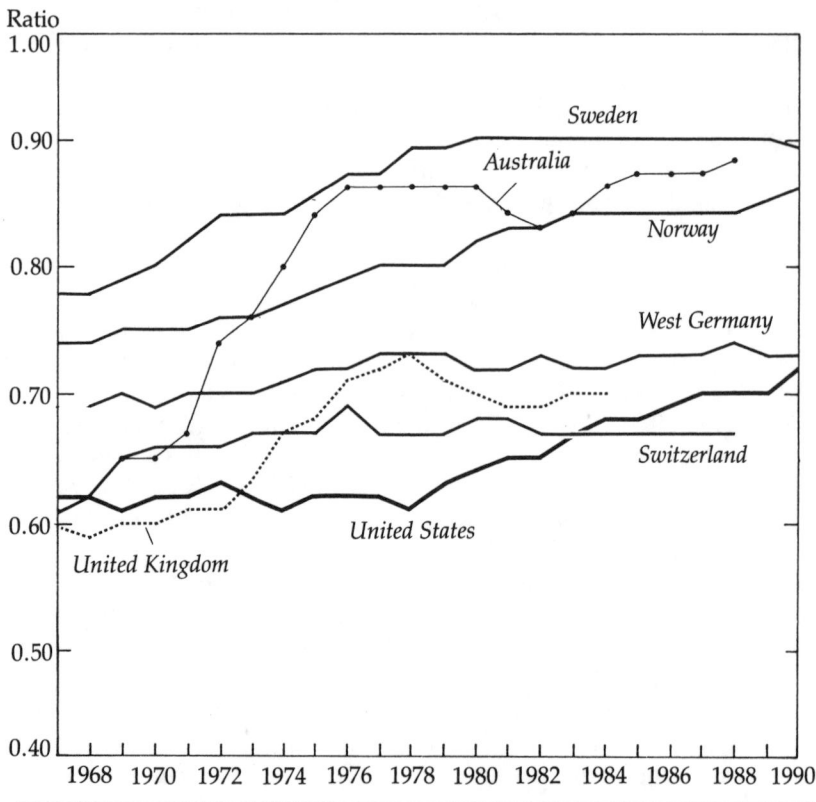

compare wages at the ninetieth and tenth percentiles with the median (fiftieth percentile) of wage distributions. Policies and practices such as legal minimum wages or extension of wage levels set by bargaining throughout an industry sector may influence these wage measures at the low end of the distribution, and characteristics of nonwage benefits may differ a great deal among countries at the top. A small decline in dispersion shown for Germany, for example, is the result of a small increase in relative wages in the bottom of the distribution that was nevertheless larger than a relative wage increase at the top. Similarly, Denmark, Italy, and Norway also experienced wider dispersion in the upper part of the distribution, but their distributions narrowed almost as much at the bottom. It is important to keep in

18

FIGURE 1–8 (continued)

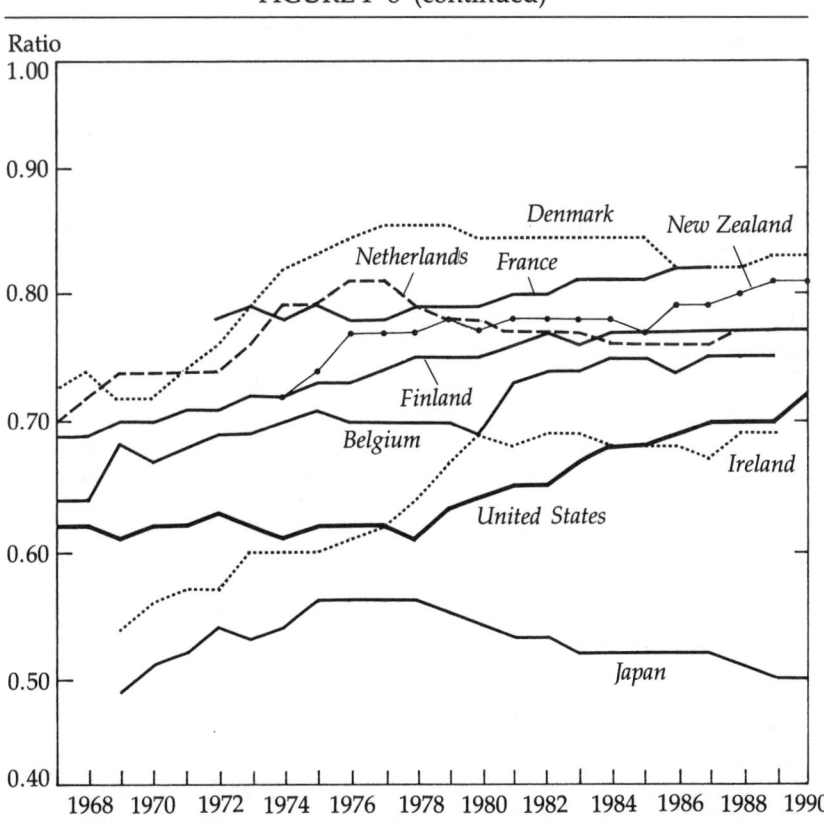

Ratio

SOURCE: Francine Blau and Lawrence Kahn, "The Gender Earnings Gap: Some International Evidence," in *Differences and Changes in Wage Structures*, Lawrence Katz and Richard Freeman, eds. (Chicago: University of Chicago Press, forthcoming).

mind the limitations of these measures of changes in the shapes of wage distributions in interpreting these results.

Changes in wage differentials between schooling levels are shown for several countries in the second part of the table. The measures of schooling for which wage differences are compared correspond reasonably closely to those for college and high school graduates in the United States. With the exception of the Netherlands, these countries show a reversal in the 1980s of the declining wage premiums of the 1970s. Although Japan does not show an increase in the schooling premium in the 1980s, these data cover only "regular" employees. A rise in the college premium for recent

19

TABLE 1-1

PATTERNS OF CHANGE IN EARNINGS DISPERSION, EDUCATION WAGE
PREMIUMS, AND WORK EXPERIENCE PREMIUMS IN SIXTEEN COUNTRIES IN THE
1970s AND 1980s

	Dispersion[a]		Education[b]		Work Experience[c] Change from
	1970s	1980s	1970s	1980s	1970s to 1980s
Australia	−	+	−.17	.03	0.09
Austria	−	+			
Belgium		+			
Canada	0	+	−.13	.03	0.14
Denmark		0			
France	−	−/+			0.14
Germany	0	−		.10	0.42
Italy	−	0			
Japan		+	−.04	0.00	0.06
Netherlands	0	−/+		−.35	0.12
Norway		0			
Portugal		+			
Spain	− −/0	+			
Sweden	0	0/+	−.09	.03	0.01
United Kingdom	−	+ +	−.06	.08	0.06
United States	+	+ +	−.08	.09	0.13

a. + = increase in dispersion; + + = strong increase; − = decrease;
− − = strong decrease; 0 = no clear change; −/+ = decrease followed by
increase; blank = information not available.
b. Five-year average change in the ratio of earnings of college-level workers
to high school–level workers.
c. Five-year average change calculated for the ratio of peak earnings (40–49
or 45–49 years old) to earnings of 25–29-year-olds.
SOURCES: *Employment Outlook*, July 1993, Organization for European Cooperation and Development. Tables 5.1, 5.5, and 5.6. Also, Davis, Steven J. "Cross-
Country Patterns of Change in Relative Wages." NBER Working Paper no.
4085, June 1992.

graduates is shown by some other studies. Finally, experience in the
United States and the United Kingdom is more closely comparable to
that of other countries in these comparisons of increases in schooling
wage premiums than in the dispersion measures.

The steepening of age-earnings profiles from the 1970s to the

1980s is shown in the right-hand column of the table. These data in general compare five-year increases in the ratio of earnings of workers in their forties with those of twenty-five- to twenty-nine–year-olds. Changes are generally computed from earlier troughs, some of which occurred well before the 1980s. These increases in the slopes of age-earnings profiles were quite widespread, extending even to France, Germany, and the Netherlands, which by some of the other measures show little change in wage patterns over the years. These increases in work experience wage premiums for the United States and the United Kingdom are also more or less comparable in size with those in most other countries.

In their review of increases in wage inequality across countries, Richard B. Freeman and Lawrence F. Katz (1993) place considerable emphasis on the much larger increases in dispersion in the United States and the United Kingdom than in other advanced countries. Although they view these other countries as facing labor-market pressures similar to those affecting the United States and the United Kingdom, the effects on dispersion seem to have been mitigated by various national policies. Comparatively weak employment growth and increases in long-term unemployment in many of these countries may be partly attributable to these policies to counter labor-market pressures that would otherwise have produced more wage inequality.

The OECD comments as follows on the international comparisons of wage dispersion they review and summarize:

> The observed consistency between the changes in dispersion in such a wide range of countries, especially with regard to the contrast between the 1970s and 1980s, suggests that pervasive economic factors are at work. This hypothesis is strengthened by another fact: those countries which did not experience an increase in dispersion over the 1980s, Denmark, Finland, Germany, Italy, and Norway, are countries where national institutions have a particularly strong influence on wage setting and may have masked the effects of demographic and economic forces.[6]

Comparisons among countries have also been made of the extent to which increases in dispersion have been associated with changes in wages between industries or within industry sectors. These comparisons for Australia, Canada, France, Japan, the Netherlands, Sweden, the United Kingdom, and the United States all show that changes in dispersion have been predominantly concentrated within industries. Increased dispersion has apparently not been a result of

---

6. Ibid., p. 166.

shifts in employment from manufacturing to services, for example, as has often been suggested in popular discussion. Rather it has resulted from increased dispersion within relatively narrow industry sectors.[7]

Sources of Changes in Wage Patterns

Several studies have examined potential sources of changes in wage patterns. Some studies have used formal methods to trace measures of wage behavior, such as the college–high school premium, to various possible sources. Others have examined wage relationships and descriptive information that may provide clues about the likely importance of various factors. The results of these studies are summarized below by first reviewing data on changes in supply. Then the possible influence of a number of government policies and institutional factors is discussed. Finally, factors influencing demand are examined: specifically, the potential roles of technology and trade.

Labor Supply

Since education and work experience are important determinants of workers' earning capabilities, we might expect that changes in relative proportions of workers with particular education and experience qualifications would affect their relative wages. To estimate the influence on wage patterns of changes in supply, therefore, it is natural to begin by examining changes in the age and schooling mix of the work force. The combination of the rising rate of school enrollment among youth, particularly beyond high school, and the large increase in the numbers who attained working age in the 1970s and 1980s led to unusually large changes in relative supply. Some characteristics of these changes for the working-age population of the United States are illustrated in figure 1–9 for some simple but crude measures of changes in the schooling and work experience mix.[8] Patterns of change are broadly similar for totals to those for white males only.

The first panel of the figure shows changes in the fraction of youth (twenty- to twenty-nine–year-olds) who have completed twelve and sixteen years of schooling, described as high school and college graduates, respectively. Many of the twenty- to twenty-two–year-

---

7. Ibid., table 5.8, p. 173.

8. These data are essentially the same as those presented in a series of figures by Mincer (1993), chapter 13. I have updated the data and reported them in a slightly different form, but they tell much the same story.

FIGURE 1–9

PROPORTIONS OF HIGH SCHOOL AND COLLEGE GRADUATES IN THE UNITED
STATES FOR SELECTED AGE CATEGORIES, 1964–1991

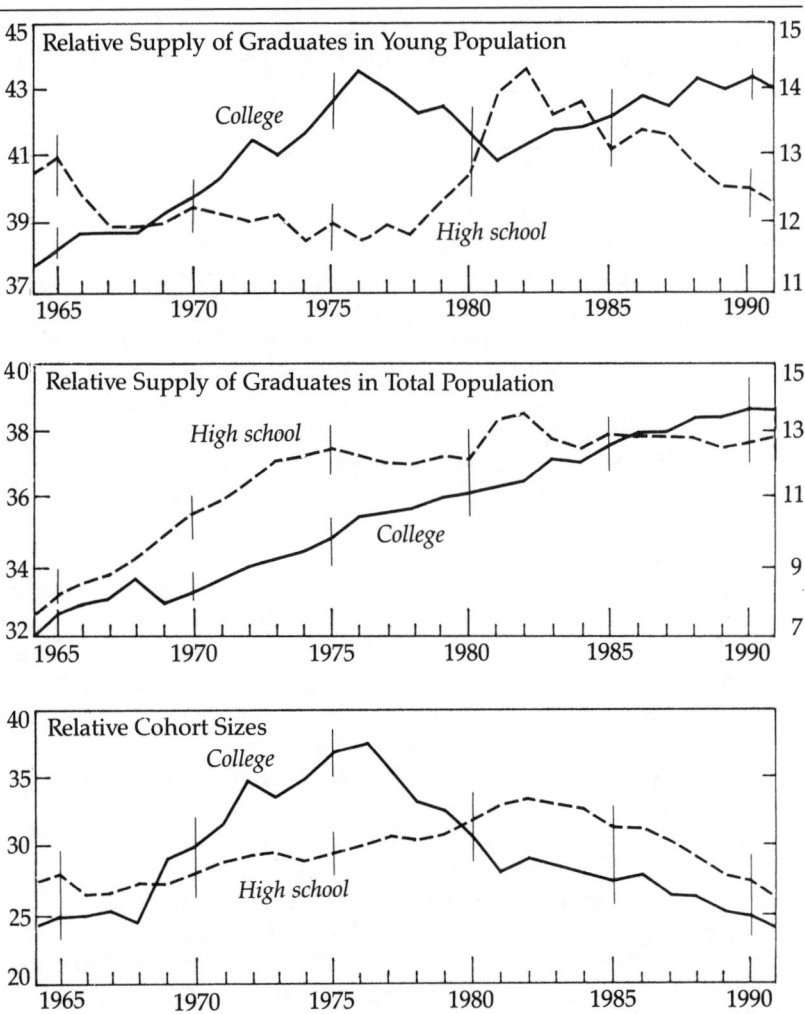

NOTE: The scales for the first two panels of this figure measure the percentage of high school graduates on the left axis and the percentage of college
graduates on the right. For the last panel, the percentage of graduates at
both levels is measured on the left-hand scale.
SOURCE: Author's computations; data from U.S. Bureau of the Census.

olds included in this age category, and some who are older, have not yet completed college, although they would soon be college graduates. These data on youth show a sharp rise in the fraction who graduated from college from the mid-1960s to 1976, followed by a slump until 1981 and a subsequent recovery to the peak levels of the mid-1970s. After a decline to 1967, the fraction with high school was stable until 1978, increased sharply to 1982, and then declined back to about its starting level. These fluctuations are important because this youth cohort composes such a large share of the work force during most of these years.

For the working-age population as a whole, the effect on the schooling mix of the youth bulge is dominated by the size of the group of young people instead of the schooling they obtained, as shown in the second panel of the figure. Thus, from the late 1960s to the late 1970s the high school share of the working-age population increased by more than the college share, even though the share of young people obtaining four years of college was relatively high. The huge increase in the college–high school wage premium during the 1980s (see figure 1–6) may seem surprising in view of the steady increase in the proportion of working-age people with college and the stable proportion with high school.

The third panel charts the fractions of working-age high school and college graduates who are young. It shows a sharp increase in the youth share of college graduates from 1968 to 1976. In their peak years, these young people accounted for more than a third of all working-age college graduates. The baby boom added many college graduates to a relatively small pool in the first half of the 1970s. Since the pool of high school graduates was much larger and the fraction of youth only attending high school was declining, the youth share of high school graduates rose more slowly. The youth share of college graduates peaked earlier than for high school graduates, a trend that may be related to the earlier rise in the work-experience wage premium for college graduates shown in the second panel of figure 1–6. After attaining their peaks, youth shares declined gradually for both groups as smaller numbers of baby boom youth were added to pools that had already grown larger. Changes in the schooling mix as schooling levels were upgraded over the years had little effect on the wage structure, however, compared with changes in schooling-wage premiums.

Some of the changes in work experience and schooling-wage premiums in the 1970s and 1980s can be traced to changes in relative supply.[9] But supply changes defined in terms of schooling and work

9. See, for example, Katz and Murphy (1992).

experience cannot account for the whole story. This was demonstrated formally by Murphy and Welch (1988), who examined relationships between wages and the age and schooling mix of the white male work force to see whether patterns of wage change could be consistent with relative supply changes only.[10] Based on the detailed age and schooling categories they used, they concluded that sign patterns were consistent with a stable demand structure from 1963 to 1981. After 1981, however, the pattern of signs was not consistent with stable demand; demand patterns must have changed in the 1980s. Rising demand for workers with college-level training is illustrated by the continued rise in the share of college graduates (shown in the second panel of figure 1–9) during the 1980s, when the college-wage premium rose sharply (as shown in the first panel of figure 1–6). Increases in the relative supply of college-level workers were smaller in the 1980s than in the 1970s, not only in the United States but in most other industrial countries as well.

A deterioration in schooling quality at the elementary and secondary level relative to college-level schooling could be another potential source of an effective change in relative supply. The rise in the college-wage premium during the 1980s came at a time when concerns about the quality of schooling at the elementary and secondary levels were widely publicized. Although test scores suggest that quality deterioration may have been a factor, other evidence indicates that its effects must have been relatively small.[11] Comparisons of the size of increases in college-wage premiums by vintage of schooling, for workers who acquired their schooling in earlier years relative to more recent graduates, clearly show that these wage premiums were not sensitive to such differences in timing. *When* schooling was acquired had little effect on the size of college premiums compared with differences in schooling *levels*, whenever they were attained.

Immigration is also a source of possible change in relative supply. Although the effects of immigration are presumably already reflected in data on the age and schooling mix of the work force from sources based on surveys of residents, their contribution to changes in wage patterns can nevertheless be considered separately. Evidence suggests that immigration had a noticeable influence on measures of relative wage change for small components of the work force, such as workers who did not complete high school, perhaps in part because

---

10. This analysis is also summarized in Murphy and Welch (1991, 1992).

11. Bishop (1991) examines the evidence from data on measures of achievement. Blackburn, Bloom, and Freeman (1990), Kosters (1991), and Murphy and Welch (1993b) compare changes in wage patterns for cohorts.

this component is quite small and many of these immigrants may also have had language limitations.[12] It is fairly clear from evidence for the work force as a whole, however, that increasing immigration during the 1980s could account for only a small proportion of the rise in schooling-wage premiums in the United States.[13] Until recently, immigration has not been very significant in most European countries.

Government Policy and Wage-setting Institutions

Government policy could affect wage patterns in several ways. Some policies, such as deregulation, influence competition in the marketplace. Others, such as legal minimum wages, directly constrain the degree to which wages are allowed to respond to labor market forces. Wage-setting institutions have also been subject to varying degrees of government influence. The role of institutions may also have changed in some instances in response to changes in the economic environment.

Deregulation (especially in the United States) and privatization (perhaps especially in the United Kingdom) may have influenced wage structures. The main direct influence of these policies is on competition in product markets. But changes in derived demand for labor that resulted could influence wages in industries most directly affected, and secondary effects on other industries might occur. Deregulation of transportation industries—trucking, airlines, railroads, and intercity buses—and of telecommunications in the United States had effects on wage setting in many of these industries, such as lower wage scales for new employees. The effects of deregulation and of pushing previously nationalized industries into the marketplace may have contributed to decentralization of wage setting in these industries. Most of the increase in wage dispersion took place within industries, however, instead of between industries. Although the effects of more competition are not easily quantified, deregulation may have contributed to producing wage behavior within the most strongly affected industries that was similar to wage behavior in other industries.[14]

The real level of the federal minimum wage was declining in the United States during most of the 1980s. Its estimated effects on the wage structure are small, however, in part because wages of only a

---

12. Borjas, Freeman, and Katz (1992).
13. Bound and Johnson (1991, 1992).
14. Murphy and Welch (1993b).

small proportion of the work force could have been affected by the low real federal minimum wage during much of the 1980s.[15] Moreover, a large share of the increase in wage dispersion in the United States and other countries took place in the upper part of the distribution, which is unlikely to have been significantly affected by the minimum wage. Minimum wages may have contributed, however, to mitigating increases in dispersion in some European countries, such as France, where the real minimum wage was increased during the 1980s.[16]

A reduction in the centralization of wage-setting institutions and arrangements apparently occurred in some European countries, including Sweden, during the 1980s. These changes may have provided flexibility for more market-oriented wage determination. Changes in wage patterns could as a result more fully reflect differences in supply and demand conditions and differences in circumstances among firms and industries. It is also possible, however, that the influence of decentralization was limited in many European countries because private-sector employment growth was extraordinarily sluggish during most of the 1980s compared with the United States, and increased wage dispersion has been more evident in the private than in the public sector.[17]

The decline in union density, especially in the United States but also in other countries, makes it an obvious candidate for examination. Studies of the effects of the decline in unionization suggest that its effects on wage dispersion were small and that it could account for only a small proportion of the wage structural changes that occurred.[18] Since the extent of unionism has been declining gradually since the 1950s, the timing of the changes in wage premiums and dispersion that occurred in the United States does not suggest that unionization could have played a major role for the work force as a whole. The decline in union density should also probably be regarded as largely endogenous, reflecting factors such as the decline in the manufacturing employment share and the growth of more individualized and specially tailored arrangements for wages and working

---

15. See Bound and Johnson (1991) for evidence on the limited impact of the minimum wage. See Blackburn, Bloom, and Freeman (1990) for evidence that the minimum wage might have had a small effect for high school dropouts.
16. Katz, Loveman, and Blanchflower (1993).
17. OECD (1993) and Katz and Krueger (1991).
18. See Bound and Johnson (1992), Blackburn, Bloom, and Freeman (1990), and Freeman (1993).

conditions in many industries with expanding employment shares. This raises questions about the extent to which it should be considered as an independent source of changes in the wage structure.

Government programs such as social security, disability payments, income maintenance programs, tax credits for employers, and income tax credits for workers with low earnings could influence labor force behavior in ways related to skill levels, but their actual effects are quite speculative. Similarly, differences among countries in worker training programs, especially for youth and workers with low skills, could influence labor supply and wages at the low end of the distribution. Worker training programs, such as those that involve the transition from school to work (apprenticeship), within the workplace (on-the-job training), or associated with worker displacement (trade adjustment assistance in the United States and other "active labour market policies" in OECD parlance) may be important—but virtually no evidence shows that they affect wage dispersion. For most of these policies and in most countries, changes seem to have been too modest to contribute much to wage structure changes.

Technology, Trade, and Labor Demand

Influences on the wage structure that could work through labor demand include the business cycle.[19] Cyclical expansion on the wage structure is more likely to compress than to increase dispersion. Hence the business cycle is not a likely source of increased wage dispersion during most of the 1980s, particularly in the United States and the United Kingdom, where dispersion appears to have increased most. Shifts in relative employment among industry sectors, such as the widely discussed shift in proportions of employment from manufacturing to services, also apparently contributed little to increased wage dispersion. Studies that have applied "shift-share" analysis indicate only a small contribution to increased wage dispersion from this source.[20] Analysis has shown that increased within-group dispersion—even within relatively narrow industry and demographic categories—has been much more important.[21]

Technology and trade are other demand-based potential sources of pressures that may have contributed to increased wage dispersion.

---

19. See Burtless (1990).

20. Kosters and Ross (1987), Bound and Johnson (1991), and Murphy and Welch (1993b).

21. See Dooley and Gottschalk (1984), Juhn, Murphy, and Pierce (1993), Katz, Loveman, and Blanchflower, (1993), and Murphy and Welch (1993b).

Both the speed and the character of advances in technology are potentially relevant. Growing competition from international trade and the growth of the U.S. trade deficit in the 1980s—which displaced production in some (especially manufacturing) sectors and replaced it with production and employment expansion in others (especially services)—have been considered as possible sources of increased dispersion. It may also be difficult to disentangle technology and trade as possible sources, because, for example, increased competition from international trade could stimulate more rapid technological change and consequent changes in production processes.

Studies of the role of technological change typically examine it as a source of a bias toward increased skill demands. Jacob Mincer's 1993 analysis of schooling and work experience wage premiums, for example, suggests that research-and-development expenditures per worker, along with growth in the proportion of employment in services, performs better in explaining schooling-wage differentials than do productivity growth indexes or growth of net goods imports.[22] Eli Berman, John Bound, and Zvi Griliches (1993) use measures of R&D expenditures to show that more R&D is associated with larger declines in production-worker shares within relatively narrow industry categories—a finding that relates growth in within-group wage dispersion to technological change. Other related clues involve the role of computers: Berman, Bound, and Griliches find that investment in computers is associated with larger shrinkage in production-worker shares among industries, and Krueger (1993) finds that people who work with computers earn significantly higher wages. Bound and Johnson's 1992 study of a range of possible sources of change in the wage structure also concludes that growth in technology is likely to be the most important source of the bias toward higher skills in labor demand. These studies, and others that have examined high-tech manufacturing processes, strongly suggest that growing technological sophistication in production processes is an important source of skill upgrading within industries. New technology appears not only to be labor-saving: it also apparently reduces demand for less skilled, production worker–level labor, as compared with more skilled labor.

Skill demands in the domestic labor market could also be influenced by international trade. Relative supplies of skilled and unskilled workers differ a great deal among countries. The size of trade flows and trade imbalances has generally been larger among

---

22. See the discussion of this research by Bhagwati and Dehejia in the following chapter.

countries with skill compositions similar to ours than among countries with radically different skill compositions. The presumption in some analyses and much popular discussion, however, has been that increased exposure to trade competition has come primarily from trade with countries that are relatively abundant in low-skilled workers, compared with the United States. Under these circumstances, growth in trade could reduce relative demand for less skilled workers in the domestic labor market.

Several studies have examined the role of international trade by considering the implicit labor skill content of the domestic production displaced by growth in the trade deficit. These studies translate the implicit augmentation of the relative supply of less skilled workers into a corresponding adjustment in the domestic labor supply.[23] The evidence from these studies has been interpreted as consistent with the hypothesis that the increase in the trade deficit in the 1980s contributed importantly to the increase in the wage premium for schooling and other relative wage shifts in the United States.

A 1992 study by Ana L. Revenga examines the influence on domestic employment and wage patterns of international competition as it is reflected by import prices. She reports evidence of significant effects on industry employment and wages in the United States. George E. Johnson and Frank P. Stafford (1993), on the other hand, examined the potential influence of growth in international trade on U.S. wage levels. The framework they sketch out and the clues they provide suggest that trade might have influenced mainly real wage levels in the United States instead of the structure of relative wages.

Two related aspects of wage trends seem particularly important in considering analyses of the effects of trade on wages: the industry pattern of increases in wage dispersion, and the kinds of changes in the structure of wages that might be explained by trade. Both aspects raise questions about the evidence on the role of trade and the limitations of traditional methods of analysis.

Analyses of relationships between trade and wage patterns have relied heavily on the differential impact among industries of increases in trade or trade deficits. The influence of trade on wage patterns is presumed to result from differences in factor content between industries whose output is partially displaced by imports, and production

---

23. See Borjas, Freeman, and Katz (1992), Bound and Johnson (1991), Murphy and Welch (1991), and Katz and Murphy (1992), and see the chapter in this volume by Deardorff and Hakura for a careful evaluation of these and other studies.

is therefore forced to contract, and other industries that use the resources that are released to expand and produce output for other domestic or export markets. Changes in the structure of wages that can be traced to changes in wage patterns among industries differentially affected by trade would suggest possible trade effects. Since most of the increase in wage dispersion is accounted for by increases within industries instead of between industries, however, only a small proportion remains that could be traced in part to trade effects.[24] Changes in relative wages set in motion by trade in industries that are most affected could have spread quickly to other industries, of course, but this would preclude estimation of trade effects on the basis of differences in factor content among industries.

Whether growth in the trade deficit is a likely source of change in the U.S. wage structure depends in part on just what seems to call for explanation. The trend of schooling-wage premiums suggests that the 1980s brought a sharp break from previous experience. The trend of within-group wage dispersion, however, suggests that developments in the 1980s represent mainly a continuation of trends evident in the 1970s. The trend toward increased wage dispersion, under this interpretation, was temporarily obscured by the extraordinary growth in college-level labor market entrants during the 1970s and the decline in schooling-wage premiums that resulted. The trend toward increased wage dispersion reemerged in the 1980s, partly in response to the slowdown in the rate at which schooling levels were upgraded. The effect of the underlying skill bias in labor demand growth was temporarily interrupted by rapid growth in one dimension of labor market skills—schooling—even though returns to other dimensions of skill continued to rise. After the effects of these supply changes are taken into account, what has to be explained is the longer-term growth in skill demands, and the rise in within-group wage dispersion that resulted. The turnaround in returns to schooling in the 1980s corresponds more closely in timing to the growth of the trade deficit.

Although the United Kingdom experienced changes in its wage structure more or less similar in size and pattern to those in the United States, developments in its trade balances were very different. The U.S. current account balance became negative in 1982 and reached a peak of about 3.6 percent of GDP in 1987, while the current account deficit for the United Kingdom emerged in 1987 and increased rapidly during the next two years to about 4 percent of GDP before declining.

---

24. Murphy and Welch (1993b).

Concluding Comments

The main characteristics of changes in wage patterns that occurred during the 1980s and earlier were summarized at the beginning of this chapter. Some brief comments on the causes of these changes may help set the stage for a careful examination of the role of international trade.

A number of factors have been examined in studies of the sources of changes in the structure of wages. These factors include changes in the composition of employment by industry, the education and age mix of the work force, schooling quality, worker training, minimum-wage policy, wage-setting institutions, union density, immigration, business-cycle developments, and regulatory policies. Some of these factors, such as immigration and union density, apparently made some contribution to changes in the wage structure. Others, such as possible changes in schooling quality and business-cycle developments, seem to have made little or no contribution. The main conclusion I draw from these studies is that taken together, these factors account for only a small portion of the pronounced changes in the structure of wages that took place in the U.S. labor market.

Changes in the wage structure can evidently be traced in part to shifts in the schooling and work experience composition of the labor force. The influence of these supply shifts on the wage structure was primarily attributable to their effects on relative wages—the prices set by the labor market for workers' skills. Since they cannot by themselves account for the observed changes in wage structure, however, these supply shifts must have been accompanied by changes in demand from sources such as technology or trade. The evidence suggests that technological change could be a major source of rising skill premiums, but this evidence is necessarily indirect in view of the limitations of measures of technology likely to be most relevant for the labor market. Studies of the influence of trade raise issues that are addressed in detail in the following two chapters.

Selected References

Berman, Eli, John Bound, and Zvi Griliches. "Changes in the Demand for Skilled Labor within U.S. Manufacturing Industries: Evidence from the Annual Survey of Manufacturing." National Bureau of Economic Research (NBER) Working Paper no. 4255, January 1993.

Bishop, John. "Achievement, Test Scores, and Relative Wages." In Marvin Kosters, ed., *Workers and Their Wages*. Washington, D.C.: AEI Press, 1991.

Blackburn, McKinley L., David E. Bloom, and Richard B. Freeman. "The Declining Economic Position of Less Skilled American Men." In Gary Burtless, ed., *A Future of Lousy Jobs?* Brookings Institution, 1990.

Blau, Francine D., and Lawrence M. Kahn, "The Gender Earnings Gap: Some International Evidence." NBER Working Paper no. 4224, 1992.

———. "The Gender Earnings Gap: Some International Evidence." In Lawrence Katz and Richard Freeman, eds., *Differences and Changes in Wage Structures*. Chicago, Ill.: University of Chicago Press, forthcoming.

Bluestone, Barry. "The Impact of Schooling and Industrial Restructuring on Recent Trends in Wage Inequality in the United States." *American Economic Review Proceedings*, May 1990.

Borjas, George, Richard B. Freeman, and Lawrence F. Katz. "On the Labor Market Effects of Immigration and Trade." In George Borjas and Richard Freeman, eds., *Immigration and the Work Force*. University of Chicago and NBER, 1992.

Bound, John, and George Johnson. "Wages in the United States during the 1980s and Beyond." In Marvin Kosters, ed., *Workers and Their Wages*. Washington, D.C.: AEI Press, 1991.

———. "Changes in the Structure of Wages in the 1980s." *American Economic Review*, June 1992.

Burtless, Gary. "Earnings Inequality over the Business and Demographic Cycles." In Gary Burtless, ed., *A Future of Lousy Jobs?* The Brookings Institution, Washington, D.C., 1990.

Card, David, and Alan Krueger. "School Quality and Black-White Relative Earnings: A Direct Assessment." NBER Working Paper no. 3713, 1991.

Danziger, Sheldon, and Peter Gottschalk, eds., *Uneven Tides: Rising Inequality in America*. Russell Sage Foundation, 1993.

Davis, Steven J. "Cross-Country Patterns of Change in Relative Wages." NBER Working Paper no. 4085, June 1992.

Dooley, Martin, and Peter Gottschalk. "Earnings Inequality among Males in the United States: Trends and the Effect of Labor Force Growth." *Journal of Political Economy*, February 1984.

Edin, Per-Anders, and Bertil Holmlund. "The Swedish Wage Structure: The Rise and Fall of Solidarity Wage Policy?" NBER Working Paper no. 4257, January 1993.

Freeman, Richard B. "How Much Has De-Unionization Contributed to the Rise in Male Earnings Inequality?" In Sheldon Danziger, and Peter Gottschalk, eds., *Uneven Tides*. Russell Sage Foundation, 1993.

————. *The Overeducated American.* New York: Academic Press, 1976.

Freeman, Richard B., and Lawrence F. Katz. "Rising Wage Inequality: The United States versus Other Advanced Countries." NBER Conference Paper, May 7, 1993.

Goldin, Claudia, and Robert A. Margo. "The Great Compression: The Wage Structure in the United States at Mid-Century." *Quarterly Journal of Economics*, February 1992.

Johnson, George E., and Frank P. Stafford. "International Competition and Real Wages." *American Economic Review*, May 1993.

Juhn, Chinhui, Kevin M. Murphy, and Brooks Pierce. "Accounting for the Slowdown in Black-White Wage Convergence." In Marvin Kosters, ed., *Workers and Their Wages*. Washington, D.C.: AEI Press, 1991.

————. "Wage Inequality and the Rise in Returns to Skill." *Journal of Political Economy*, June 1993.

Katz, Lawrence F., and Alan Krueger. "Changes in the Structure of Wages in the Public and Private Sectors." NBER Working Paper no. 3667, 1991.

Katz, Lawrence F., Gary Loveman, and David Blanchflower. "A Comparison of Changes in the Structure of Wages in Four OECD Countries." NBER Working Paper no. 4297, 1993.

Katz, Lawrence F., and Kevin M. Murphy. "Changes in Relative Wages, 1963–1987: Supply and Demand Factors." *Quarterly Journal of Economics*, February 1992.

Katz, Lawrence F., and Ana L. Revenga. "Changes in the Structure of Wages: The U.S. versus Japan." NBER Working Paper no. 3021, July 1989.

Kosters, Marvin H. "Wages and Demographics." In Marvin Kosters, ed., *Workers and Their Wages*. Washington, D.C.: AEI Press, 1991.

Kosters, Marvin H., and Murray L. Ross. "The Influence of Employment Shifts and New Job Opportunities on the Growth and Distribution of Real Wages." In Philip Cagan, ed., *Deficits, Taxes, and Economic Adjustments*. Washington, D.C.: American Enterprise Institute, 1987.

Krueger, Alan B. "How Computers Have Changed the Wage Structure: Evidence from Microdata, 1984–1989." *Quarterly Journal of Economics*, vol. 108, Feb. 1993, pp. 33–60.

Lawrence, Robert Z., and Matthew J. Slaughter. "International Trade and American Wages in the 1980s: Giant Sucking Sound or Small Hiccup?" *Brookings Papers on Economic Activity*, vol. 2, 1993, Microeconomics, pp. 161–226.

Levy, Frank, and Richard J. Murnane. "U.S. Earnings Levels and Earnings Inequality: A Review of Recent Trends and Proposed Explanations." *Journal of Economic Literature*, September 1992.

Lynch, Lisa M. "Payoffs to Alternate Training Strategies at Work." NBER Conference Paper, May 7, 1993.

Mincer, Jacob. *Schooling, Experience, and Earnings.* New York: Columbia University Press, 1974.

———. *Studies in Human Capital: Collected Essays of Jacob Mincer,* vol. 1. Hampshire, England: Edward Elgar, 1993.

Murphy, Kevin M. and Finis Welch. "The Structure of Wages." Unicon Research, November 1988.

———. "The Role of International Trade in Wage Differentials." In Marvin Kosters, ed., *Workers and Their Wages.* Washington, D.C.: AEI Press, 1991.

———. "The Structure of Wages." *Quarterly Journal of Economics,* February 1992.

———. "Inequality and Relative Wages." *American Economic Review,* May 1993 [1993a].

———. "Industrial Change and the Rising Importance of Skill." In Sheldon Danzinger and Peter Gottschalk, eds., *Uneven Tides.* Russell Sage Foundation, 1993 [1993b].

OECD. "Employment/Unemployment Study Interim Report by the Secretary-General." OCDE/GD(93)102. Paris, France: 1993.

———. *Employment Outlook.* Paris, France: July 1993.

Revenga, Ana L. "Exporting Jobs: The Impact of Import Competition on Employment and Wages in U.S. Manufacturing." *Quarterly Journal of Economics,* February 1992.

2
Freer Trade and Wages of the Unskilled—Is Marx Striking Again?

Jagdish Bhagwati
and
Vivek H. Dehejia

Where does the threat to free trade come from today? Not from the developments in the theory of imperfect competition in product markets that defined the scientific revolution in trade theory in the 1980s. That revolution is now absorbed, and its major figures have returned to the fold of free trade, as leaders of other such revolutions have done before them (Bhagwati 1992). Instead, there are now, in our judgment, two new threats, each posing great danger.

The first threat comes from the proliferation of demands for fair trade or level playing fields as preconditions for free trade. Where

This chapter was prepared for the Workshop on Trade and Wages at the American Enterprise Institute, September 10, 1993. It draws, and builds, on earlier work by Bhagwati (1991a) done at the Russell Sage Foundation, whose financial support in 1990 and 1991 is gratefully acknowledged. In that work, the contention that trade was depressing the real wages of the unskilled was first challenged by using the general-equilibrium (Stolper-Samuelson) argumentation of trade theory to analyze the claims to that effect in the emerging labor-economists' studies of the question. An alternative explanation of a possible adverse impact of trade on wages was also advanced, in terms of the effect of an increased randomization of comparative advantage in different manufactures leading to more rapid turnover among them by the unskilled, resulting in the reduction of incremental rewards due to staying on the job longer. The chapter also draws on work by Dehejia (1992b), who models the alternative approach just described. In revising this work, we have profited from the comments of the workshop participants, especially of Susan Collins. Conversations with Douglas Irwin, Paul Samuelson, T. N. Srinivasan, Arvind Panagariya, and Martin Wolf were helpful.

conventionally such demands were confined to foreign subsidies and predatory dumping, they have now multiplied to a variety of domestic policies and institutions, including environmental and labor standards and technology policy. The presumption today is that diversity among countries in these domestic policies is harmful to the case for free trade and that free trade with such diversity, instead of being mutually beneficial, will lead to predation at one's expense. The difficulty of achieving harmonization of these several domestic policies (even in the European Community, where political congruence is far greater than among nations trading at arm's length) and the ease with which such demands can be multiplied to new areas of diversity by protectionists make the task of liberalizing trade or maintaining open markets that much more difficult.[1] The problems that the North American Free Trade Agreement (NAFTA) has run into with the environmentalists and the labor unions in the United States because of different and lower environmental and labor standards in Mexico; the strong opposition to the General Agreement on Tariffs and Trade (GATT) and to the Uruguay Round's completion around the Dunkel Draft by the environmental nongovernmental organizations (NGOs); the Clinton administration's capture by the Japan-fixated revisionists; and the surrender of key administration economists to demands for managed trade because Japan's domestic institutions are "different," and allegedly lead to a lack of level playing fields for market access, are a reminder of the grave importance the question of fair trade has acquired today.

But the other issue that imperils free trade is the fear that has grown in the United States and in Western Europe that the freeing of trade with the poor countries of the South will hurt the real wages of the unskilled. The Russian proverb warns, Fear has big eyes. But the fear in this instance is prompted by the stagnation of U.S. proletarian wages in the 1980s and the substantial increase in European unemployment, which has presumably substituted for the fall in wages,

---

1. Bhagwati (1991c), in the Harry Johnson Lecture on *The World Trading System at Risk*, identified this as one of the major problems confronting the world trading system today. Subsequently, Ford Foundation has supported a major project on the subject of Fairness Claims and Gains from Trade, addressed precisely to the question of the virtues and vices of diversity (in domestic policies and institutions among trading nations), directed by him and Professor Robert Hudec of Minnesota Law School. Nearly thirty international and other economic theorists, international lawyers, and political scientists wrote analytically oriented papers with policy implications. The findings were presented at a June 1994 conference in Washington, D.C., organized by the American Society for International Law.

during the same period. There is real cause for worry. At a time when the capacity of the Western states to maintain, leave aside raise, social expenditures to countervail the market-determined declines in real wages has been crippled (as witness the fate of the original Clinton budget proposals), and when the declinist rhetoric of the election campaign reinforced pessimism about the American economy's future, it is not surprising that workers have become fearful of real wage stagnation or decline and, with it, of trade which they believe (but without good cause, as we will suggest) is an important, if not the main, cause of this baleful phenomenon. While Karl Marx's prediction of the immiseration of the proletariat was proven wrong by history, will he strike again now through the integration of the North with the South in freer trade?[2]

Indeed, it is curious that there has been a reversal of attitudes between the countries of the North and those of the South when trade between them is appraised. During the 1950s and 1960s, much of the South regarded trade with the North as a threat, not as an opportunity, was fearful that without protection it could not industrialize, and turned to import substitution while the North was opening to the South (as to itself) through extensive liberalization. Today, starting with the 1980s, there have been fearful voices in the North, dreading trade with the poor South as a recipe for descent into the wages and working conditions of these impoverished nations. Many in the South, conversely, see trade with the North as an opportunity, not a peril. The contrast between Mexico's and the U.S. Congress's reaction to NAFTA is a stark example of this role reversal.[3]

In this chapter, we want to address this fear, prevalent in the North. There is little prospect that we can get much farther toward free trade if this issue is not addressed clearly and persuasively. In this chapter, we will not present original empirical work, but instead will clarify the issues from the viewpoint of international trade theory and relate the arguments to empirical evidence available from others'

---

2. Scholars of Marx are, of course, divided over the question whether, in addition to his prediction of a falling rate of profit, Marx did indeed predict a falling real wage for the proletariat. But enough scholars, and much of the public, believe that he did, justifying our allusion above.

3. We speak in aggregate terms of fears and opinions, fully aware that there are exceptions to the fears of trade in the North (indeed, in the U.S. Congress on NAFTA as well) and to the embrace of trade as an opportunity in the South (as among leftist political parties in India). Nonetheless, the central thrust of intellectual and policy-making opinion has changed favorably in much of the South, and the fears have grown, though not yet overturning policy, in much of the North.

studies. Directions for future research should emerge from our analysis.

Factor Price Equalization—A Theoretical Curiosum or Inescapable Destiny?

Interestingly, the major theoretical construct which, implicitly or explicitly, has provided the intellectual support, and lent the air of plausibility, to the fears in the North of immiseration of the unskilled from freer trade with the South has been the celebrated factor price equalization (FPE) theorem (and the Stolper-Samuelson [SS] theorem which shows the adverse impact of free trade on the factor of production that is scarce in the country relative to abroad in the country's trading partners—that is, presumably unskilled labor in the North vis-à-vis unskilled labor in the South, relative to other factors of production such as capital).[4]

It is interesting, of course, that when Paul Samuelson wrote his famous pair of articles on the FPE theorem in the *Economic Journal* in 1948 and 1949, the theorem was considered at first to be implausible[5] and hence possibly wrong,[6] and then to be little more than a theoretical *curiosum*. At the same time, when Wassily Leontief (1953) came up with his startling finding that the United States was exporting labor-intensive exports, the search for explanations that was set off primarily focused on the reasons why the FPE theorem, building on the Heckscher-Ohlin-Samuelson model, would *not* hold in the real world because one or more of the sufficiency conditions (such as the

---

4. In the symmetric nxn case, the FPE theorem implies the SS theorem (as stated above), but the SS theorem does not imply the FPE theorem. In principle, it is enough to have the SS theorem to generate the fears that, if one is importing labor-intensive goods from the poor, labor-abundant South, free trade will harm the real wage of labor.

5. Paul Samuelson wrote the second article because the first one met with skepticism and the *Economic Journal* had to destroy in proof two articles, including one by the celebrated Cambridge economist Pigou, questioning the FPE theorem after Samuelson's first article appeared. Pigou remained skeptical and asked Richard Kahn if Samuelson had consulted a mathematician for his univalence proof. Informed that Samuelson was one himself, Pigou reportedly replied: I mean a British mathematician.

6. Gunnar Myrdal, and others, also found the FPE theorem implausible, because they equated the equalization of real wages in the theorem with per capita real income equalization. Obviously, the latter would still be different in the Heckscher-Ohlin-Samuelson world of identical technologies but different capital-labor endowment ratios.

absence of factor-intensity reversals) were unrealistic. In short, the approach to the FPE theorem was not that it defined reality; rather it was that the theorem provided the researcher with the necessary clues as to why it did not.

By contrast, economists have generally tended to regard FPE today as an inescapable destiny, with the unskilled proletariat facing inevitable immiseration or, at a minimum, a heavy drag on the rise of its real wages. Two examples should suffice.

The first occurred at a Williamsburg retreat for freshmen congressmen organized by the American Enterprise Institute and the Brookings Institution after the 1992 election. One of the authors, Jagdish Bhagwati, and Lester Thurow were joint panelists. In speaking about NAFTA, Thurow, an influential Democrat, reminded his audience of the economists' FPE theorem and its implications—drawing not protectionist conclusions but the prescription to raise the skills of our labor force.

For the second example, let us quote the celebrated author of FPE, Paul Samuelson himself, in a speech in Italy in 1992, adding the caveat that is is not meant to be a scholarly analysis of the matter at hand:[7]

First, any top-notch jobs that used to pay well have *not* disappeared from the face of the globe. They have merely migrated from Europe and North America to Japan, Korea, Taiwan, Singapore, Hong Kong, Malaysia, and elsewhere. (The tennis racket I play with comes from Korea. My partner plays with one made in Taiwan. These words are written on a word processor from Japan. So it goes.)

Have the jobs migrated permanently? Or will they come back? Can good governmental policies bring them back?

Last December when I attended a Nobel Jubilee, I was being driven to the Stockholm airport. Along the road we passed many of Sweden's best factories. They seemed to the tourist's eye to have lost some of their bright glitter and busy-ness. "No wonder," I thought, "that the miracle of the progressive Swedish welfare state has petered out since 1970. Now there is nothing that these factories can do which cannot be done almost as well in the Pacific Basin—and often with Asian labor at real wage rates only half that prevailing in Sweden. And surely much the same can be said about factories in Turin, Brussels, Birmingham and

---

7. Besides, the quote is only an excerpt of a speech that contains several shrewd observations on the relevance of free trade at the end of the twentieth century. See Paul Samuelson (1992).

Chicago. As Madrid and Barcelona begin to enjoy higher living standards, surely they too will begin to encounter effective competition from the developing nations that now master modern routines and have access to up-to-date technical knowledge."

Let me not exaggerate. Of course, the most resourceful Swedish and American operations can survive at some positive level. But all of us cannot be above average. As the billions of people who live in East Asia and Latin America qualify for good, modern jobs, the half billion Europeans and North Americans who used to tower over the rest of the world will find their upward progress in living standards encountering tough resistance.

But if economists find the FPE argumentation inherently plausible, as defining an inevitable pressure on the real wages of the unskilled in today's developed countries, with their presumed freer trade and further freeing of trade with the poor countries, we must not forget two countervailing arguments, one theoretical and one empirical.

The theoretical, which we develop more systematically below, simply resurrects the earlier view, albeit with more sophistication and greater evidence, that FPE's heavy hand is far more frail than currently imagined.

The empirical, at the gut level, is simply that the phenomenon of the drag on real wages of the unskilled appeared in the 1980s when the United States and the European Community were turning to protectionism instead of opening their markets extensively to the developing countries, as during the 1950s and 1960s. The same is true for the inflow of foreign investment into the United States, whether direct foreign investment (DFI) or the flip side of our current account deficit. Both show a net *increase* in augmentation of U.S. capital from foreign sources in the 1980s, both absolutely and relative to the 1950s and 1960s (Lipsey 1992). Thus, casual empiricism suggests exactly the opposite of what is generally believed! If these facts on trade barriers and foreign investment are confirmed by careful analysis, we have a paradox on our hands from the viewpoint of those who think otherwise: a paradox that could be resolved along the lines developed by us below.

But it is not just the FPE theory's seeming plausibility that has damned foreign trade with the South as a significant cause of the immiseration of the unskilled. The early presumption to that effect was also fed by notable empirical studies by leading labor economists. The study most cited, both in academic circles and in the media (see

41

Passell 1992), was the 1990 study by George Borjas, Richard Freeman, and Lawrence Katz (1992), which concluded that the 1980s had indeed seen trade affect U.S. unskilled wages adversely. While this study seemed to draw on trade-theoretic concepts (arguing that the trade had led to an effective, relative augmentation of unskilled labor supply in the United States and thus depressed its real wage), we argue below that it really did not and that their argument was insufficient for the conclusions reached.[8]

We will consider why the FPE theorem and the SS theorem generally implied by it are not quite an adequate guide to thinking about the problem at hand. We then consider in depth why the Borjas-Freeman-Katz (1992) and Kevin Murphy–Finis Welch (1991) studies, which alerted us to the adverse impact of trade on U.S. real wages, were not well grounded in general-equilibrium theory of the type that underlies the FPE and SS theorems and indeed much of conventional trade theory, thus leaving unproven their case (which implicitly drew on such reasoning).

Why FPE and SS Theorems Are Inadequate Guides to Reality

If we look at the assumptions that underlie the FPE theorem, it becomes immediately obvious that they are extraordinarily demanding. Few would find the theorem compelling as a guide to thinking about the real world if only they were familiar with these assumptions—without which the iron hand of the FPE theorem on real wages of the U.S. unskilled cannot be taken seriously.

Thus, the FPE theorem requires that technology (as also tastes) be identical across trading countries. But then, despite identical knowhow, South and North can de facto be operating in different technological worlds if the production functions, while identically shared, are characterized by possible factor intensity reversals (such that the same good, at the same goods prices, is intensive in its use of factors differently in South and North); and if the relative factor endowments are such that South and North are actually characterized by such reversals. Production functions that can lead to such reversals of factor intensity include constant elasticity of substitution (CES), where different constant elasticities of factor substitution between

---

8. In doing so, we will draw primarily on Bhagwati (1991a) (1991b). Recently, Lawrence and Slaughter (1993) have endorsed this critique in their analysis of the problem of trade and wages. Their empirical analysis provides additional evidence, supplementing that in Bhagwati and calling even more compellingly into doubt the Stolper-Samuelson argumentation.

sectors are sufficient to create such reversals.[9] Much empirical work done after the Leontief paradox alluded to above underlines the distinct possibility that such reversals, both potential and actual, are not theoretical *curiosa* at all.[10] When such reversals arise, evidently both South and North can have rising real wages of unskilled labor thanks to free trade.

Differences in technological knowhow itself can lead to a similar outcome, of course. The spread of multinationals and the rapid diffusion of technology have narrowed this possibility, but primarily among the developed countries, where convergence of knowhow has been documented by Baumol et al. (1989). Knowhow manifestly differs across North and South. One can thus readily show again the possibility that free trade will increase the real wages of unskilled labor in both South and North.

Yet another way in which technology can differ across trading countries in equilibrium is, of course, when scale effects operate. Scale economies, whether modeled in the old way to allow for perfect competition or in the new way where they lead to imperfect competition, will also enable real wages to rise in both North and South from free trade. And few would deny that scale economies are relevant.

Thus, for many reasons, the presumption that real wages in the North and the South will converge as a result of free trade can be considered unrealistic. We will develop here only three, which we consider to be particularly pertinent, and relate them to the SS theorem, assuming that the rich country is importing unskilled labor-intensive goods and exporting human and physical capital-intensive goods, and that the terms of trade improve when trade is freed. In this (2×2) version of the theorem, which is consonant with the FPE theorem, the real wage of unskilled labor falls.[11]

---

9. This was first noted by Minhas (1962) in a classic paper, based on his Stanford dissertation. In trade theorists' language, factor intensity reversal possibility means that the capital-labor ratios in the two goods will cross over at some wage-rental ratio. If factor endowments are such that the two trading groups, South and North, are on opposite sides of the cross-over, then the same good will be capital-intensive in South and labor-intensive in North in trade. That is, technology will de facto be different in equilibrium, even though technological knowhow is identical in North and South.

10. See, for instance, the extended review of such work in the early survey of trade theory in Bhagwati (1964).

11. Thus, instead of focusing on whether there is convergence of real wages in South and North, we focus directly on the question on center stage: will cheaper labor-intensive imports from the South under freer trade cause

Scale Economies. We have already indicated that scale economies can invalidate the SS theorem, causing both factors' real wages to rise. The reason is obvious: the redistributive effect that militates against the real wage of unskilled labor can be outweighed by the "lifting-all-boats" effect of scale economies on the marginal products and hence on the real wages of both factors.

The first theoretical demonstration of this phenomenon was made by Arvind Panagariya (1980), who modeled scale economies in the old way where they were external to the firm but internal to the industry. Thus we are able to work with models of perfect competition.

Elhanan Helpman and Paul Krugman (1985) established the same conclusion in the context of scale economies internal to the firm, and hence under imperfect competition. Their analysis was, however, restricted to the special case where the output per firm did not rise with trade. Thus the added gains from trade were caused by variety rather than reduced cost, because of scale. Drusilla Brown, Alan Deardorff, and Robert Stern (1993) have now produced a more general and illuminating analysis allowing for these and other effects.[12]

Diversification. The SS theorem (as also the FPE theorem) depends on the equilibriums under autarky and free trade lying in the diversification cone—that is, trade should not lead to complete specialization. When it does, the unique relationship between goods and factor prices breaks down. Although the factor prices are unique at complete specialization on a good, goods prices are manifestly not unique, because rising prices for the good will be compatible with continued specialization on it.[13]

Equally, while the SS redistributive effect operates as long as trade shifts production toward a good without causing complete specialization, once specialization is achieved it follows that any further rise in that good's (relative) price will mean that both factors will gain from it: the lifting-all-boats effect from this improvement in

---

our real wages of the unskilled to fall? In principle, of course, it is theoretically possible for the latter to occur while FPE fails: for example, the factors that militate against SS, detailed above, may hold in the South and not in the North.

12. Their Michigan CGE model, applied to Mexico, and incorporating imperfect competition due to scale economies, also predicts a rising real wage for the United States from NAFTA.

13. We are working here with the 2 × 2 version of the SS and FPE theorems. For higher dimensionality, see Ethier's (1984) fine review.

the terms of trade (implied by the rise in the relative price of the specialized good where, and in terms of which, their reward is fixed at specialization) will ensue. The net effect could be to leave both factors better off under free trade than under autarky.[14]

But this lifting-all-boats effect will help each factor proportionately to how much it consumes of the cheaper imported goods, of course. Hence it is pertinent to observe, as the work of William Cline (1990, pp. 201–206, especially table 8.3) on textiles shows and as casual empiricism suggests for other imported goods such as low-quality footwear, the groups at the bottom of the income distribution (which must include the unskilled) disproportionately spend their incomes on imported goods whose prices are heavily influenced by protection (such as the voluntary export restraints [VERs] on footwear and the Multifiber Agreement [MFA] on textiles). Deardorff and Haveman (1991) have made the complementary observation that the invoking of administered protection has been typically for industries which are *not* intensive in the incidence of poverty in their workforce, suggesting that protection so given is, in its direct effect, to the (relative) disadvantage of the industries that are, and hence of the poor.

Trade and Competition. The lifting-all-boats effect can also arise if trade means more competition and discipline, causing X-efficiency effects which may be captured analytically as Hicks-neutral technical change. If we do this, and if we assume that the effect operates throughout the economy, in both traded sectors, then clearly both factors get their real wages improving from this, countervailing and possibly reversing the fall in the real wage of the SS-impacted factor.

But, even if we were to assume that the production-function-improvement arises differentially more in the import-competing sectors, then we can see immediately from the early work on the general-equilibrium income-elasticities of supply under technical change[15]

---

14. We deliberately compare autarky with free trade because, when either of the equilibriums being compared has tariff revenues being generated, we must make assumptions about how the revenue is disposed of. Where it is assumed to be redistributed to the factors qua consumers, we must distinguish between the effect of the trade policy in question on real *wages* and real *incomes* (inclusive of revenue transfers), as in Bhagwati (1959) and subsequent analyses of the SS theorem. This distinction is clearly important in policy discussions, as noted earlier. The adverse effect on real wages of trade, if any, could be offset by fiscal policy in principle, especially if trade leads to greater income and hence greater tax capabilities.

15. See also the beautiful paper by Findlay and Grubert (1959).

that, *ceteris paribus*, the effect will be to raise the real wage of the factor intensively used in these sectors: that is, of unskilled labor in our instance.

The econometric evidence on this hypothesis is hard to find. However, Jim Levinsohn's (1993) recent work on the imports-as-competition hypothesis, while not exactly specified in the manner suggested here, is successful in testing that hypothesis with the use of Turkish industry data under near-controlled-experiment conditions. This work suggests that our specification of the effects of trade on technical change via competition may also be borne out. As in many areas we discuss in this chapter, we must confess that ideas and hypotheses outrun plausible econometric evidence, suggesting more questions than answers for empirical research.

Convergence—To Whose Real Wage? Even though we do not consider the FPE theorem (and the SS theorem) to be compelling, for the aforementioned reasons, suppose that convergence of real wages of the unskilled will occur as a result of trade between poor and rich nations. Will that then mean, as Ross Perot and Pat Choate (1993) have argued in their recent anti-NAFTA tract, that (say) NAFTA "will pit American and Mexican workers in a race to the bottom"? In short, will convergence get U.S. real wages down to the Mexican levels prior to NAFTA, or will it raise the latter up to American levels prior to NAFTA? Where will the real wages settle in each country?

In the context of NAFTA, given the relative sizes of the United States and Mexico, we would guess that goods prices will gravitate toward U.S. prices: so, then, will factor prices. For freer trade in the world economy, between South and North, a gut answer is harder to give. We need to investigate the question analytically before we can give an informed answer; to our knowledge, no such analysis exists currently. But it is clear that the widespread presumption that, in case of convergence (which we have argued need not be expected anyway), the real wages in the rich countries will gravitate down toward the levels in the South appears to be based on panic rather than logic.

Early Labor Studies. Should we nonetheless have changed our minds in light of the early labor-economists' studies, especially by Borjas-Freeman-Katz (1992) and by Murphy and Welch (1991), which attributed a definite role to international trade in explaining the unhappy behavior of the real wages of the unskilled in the 1980s?

Excellent as these studies are, our major source of dissatisfaction with them, and hence our inability to admit them as evidence in favor of the thesis they support, is that nowhere do they build on the essential fact that trade should affect goods prices in the desired direction before anything can be inferred concerning the trade-induced effects on factor rewards.[16] We will consider this by examining the Borjas-Freeman-Katz study that was available by mid-1990. It has been much cited by economists and in the media (Passell [1992], in the *New York Times*), and it has provided intellectual support to those fearful of the effects of trade on real wages of the unskilled.[17]

Borjas, Freeman, and Katz essentially compute the unskilled labor embodied in American imports (using the observed coefficients of labor use in domestic import-competing industries) and in American exports, treating the former as notional additions to and the latter as subtractions from the stock of such labor. Since imports use more unskilled labor per dollar of gross value than exports, and since the trade deficit means that imports exceed exports, this exercise yields a substantial "addition" to America's unskilled labor, thanks to its trade. Furthermore, since in view of expanding trade deficits during the 1980s this addition to the unskilled labor stock would have been accentuated, it would seem logical to conclude that trade must have contributed *pari passu* to the observed decline in the real wage of unskilled labor.[18]

This logic is indeed plausible. However, it runs into a problem.

---

16. This, of course, is at the heart of the FPE and SS theorems. Indeed, it is a central part of the general-equilibrium theory of international trade.

17. Deardorff and Hakura (1993), in chapter 3 of this volume, suggest alternative questions. For instance, if technical change saving on unskilled labor happens exogenously, would the real wages of the unskilled fall more or less if the economy were in free trade rather than in autarky? Alternatively, we could ask whether exogenous shifts in the trade offers of foreign nations in trade with us will help or harm unskilled wages—a question that can be fitted more readily into the analysis in the text, since factor prices again would change only insofar as goods prices change because of this exogenous shift in the foreign offer curve.

We should stress that, in the following critique, we define the question of the impact of trade on wages in the following policy-relevant sense (as stated in our introduction): is integration into the world economy through the reduction of trade barriers the cause of decline in the real wage of the unskilled? That is also clearly the intent of the labor economists' studies, although the ones we call "early" studies do not specify a clear question and a model that can analytically deal with it.

18. Presumably they have in mind, then, an aggregate production function with diminishing returns. See the section below on aggregate production function, however.

The only way that real wages can be affected is if, at constant (relative) factor prices, productivity increases or, with productivity change ruled out, through a change in factor prices. Since the burden of the explanation advanced is through exogenous trade changes, the analysis must presume a change in factor prices that is unrelated to productivity change or other domestic factors. But such a change in factor prices must reflect a trade-induced change in goods prices. Borjas, Freeman, and Katz should have investigated the change in goods prices, establishing that, during the period that real wages of unskilled labor fell, the (relative) price of unskilled-labor-intensive import-competing goods fell too. Else, their argument is incomplete and cannot be accepted.

Alan Deardorff and Robert Staiger (1988) have shown that, under certain conditions, a positive correlation will exist between relative changes in factor prices and relative changes in the factor content of trade. But their model still requires associated changes in goods prices. Our objection is simply that if these changes in goods prices do not conform to what is required, the observed correlation between changes in factor prices and factor content must be dismissed as spurious. As noted below, both the earlier Bhagwati (1991a) and the later Robert Lawrence–Matthew Slaughter (1993) studies show that goods prices have changed in the *opposite* direction to what is required for the SS explanation. Indeed, it is easy to see that the Borjas-Freeman-Katz technique will indicate that real wages have fallen because of trade even when they have not changed. Thus, consider the following simple analytics.

Consider figure 2–1 where, for the U.S. economy, the set of production possibilities defined on the (only) two goods M and X is OTT, with TT as the "frontier." The goods-price ratio ($P_M P_E$), which is the relative price of the two goods, is given internationally; at the outset, it is CP. Then, an efficient market economy will produce (at the tangency of the price-line with TT) at P; consumption will be at C; and balanced trade will occur with QC of imports being exchanged for PQ of exports.

In turn, the goods-price ratio will determine the factor-price ratio, as shown in figure 2–2. Assume two factors of production, high school (HS) and college (C) graduates: the former are unskilled and the latter are skilled. The importable industry is HS-intensive in the sense that it uses, at any factor prices W_{HS}/W_C, a higher proportion of HS to C in production than does X, the exportable industry. This is quite intuitive: if the industry M using HS intensively suffers a reduced price, one would expect the (relative) reward of HS to fall. This relationship is, of course, at the heart of the SS theorem.

FIGURE 2–1
CHANGE IN TRADE AS TRADE DEFICIT CHANGES

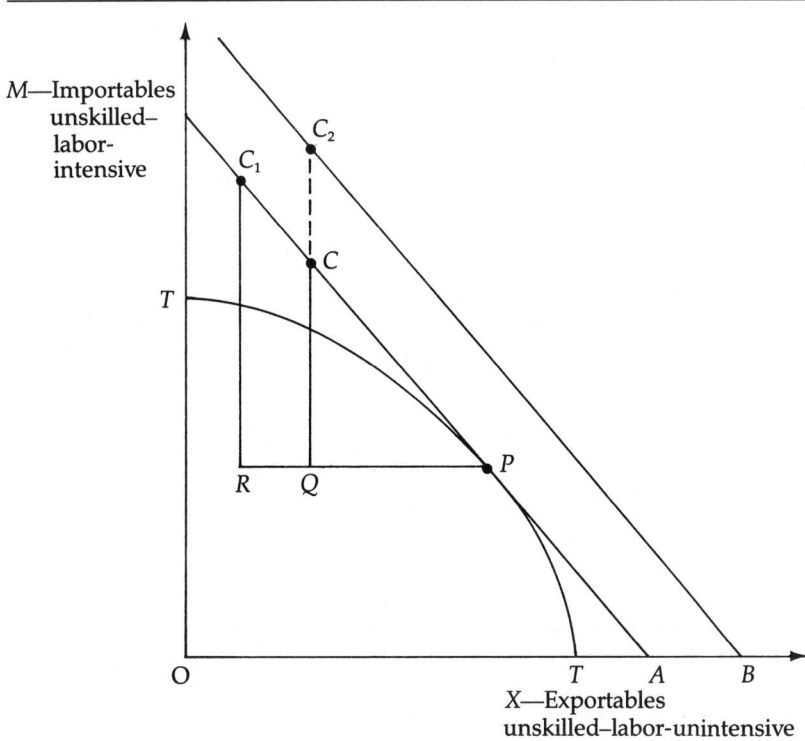

M—Importables
unskilled–
labor-
intensive

X—Exportables
unskilled–labor-unintensive

Now, return to figure 2–1. Assume that trade increases at constant goods prices (that is, without intensifying import competition), because of C shifting to C_1.[19] Imports and exports increase to C_1R and PR, respectively. The Borjas-Freeman-Katz calculation would show now an increase in the notional addition to the American stock of HS. But nothing would have happened to W_{HS}/W_C and to the real wage of HS, since the goods-price ratio has not changed.

Similarly, assume instead that the United States now runs a trade deficit so that it can spend AB more than its national income OA, measured in terms of good X. National expenditure then takes place along BC_2 instead of along the income-determined national budget line AC. Let the consumption bundle chosen then be C_2,

---

19. This could happen because of a shift in tastes, for example.

49

FIGURE 2–2
RELATIONSHIP BETWEEN GOODS-PRICE AND FACTOR-PRICE RATIOS

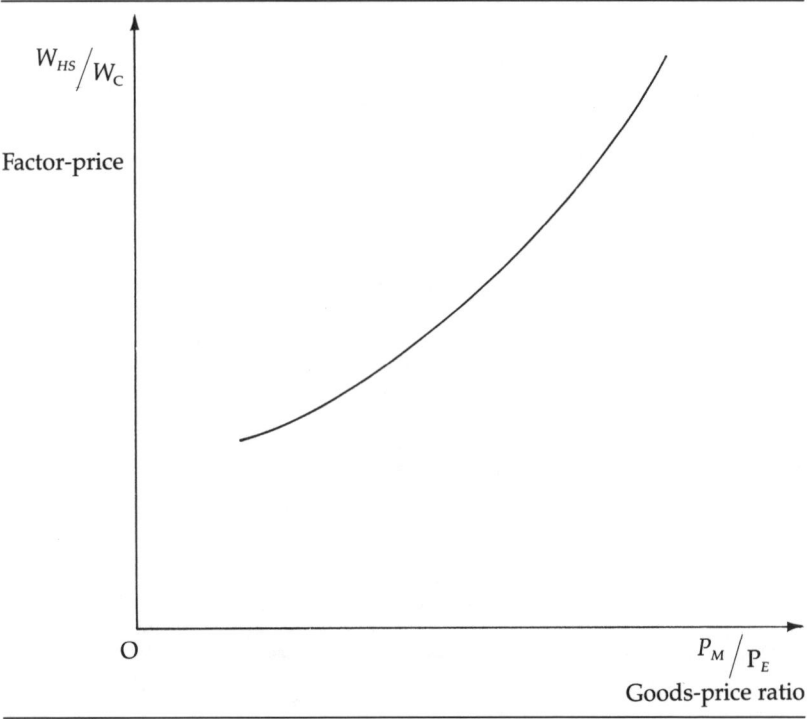

SOURCE: Authors.

implying that the deficit is associated with an equivalent increase in imports and leaves exports unchanged. The Borjas-Freeman-Katz calculation will then show again that the endowment of *HS* has gone up notionally, since *HS*-intensive imports exceed *HS*-unintensive exports by the amount of the new deficit.[20] But nothing again would have happened to W_{HS}/W_C and to the real wages of *HS* in the U.S. economy.

Thus, one cannot conclude with Borjas, Freeman, and Katz that trade in the 1980s depressed the real wages of the unskilled: their methodology can create invalid inferences to that effect. More important, they do not show that the domestic prices of the unskilled-

20. Even if we were to assume homothetic preferences, so that the consumption of both goods increases in the same proportion, exports will still fall, imports will still rise, and once again the notional endowment of *HS* will go up.

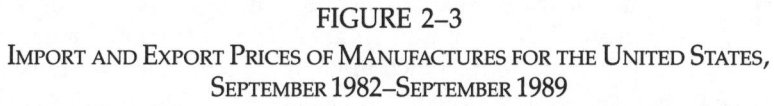

FIGURE 2–3
IMPORT AND EXPORT PRICES OF MANUFACTURES FOR THE UNITED STATES,
SEPTEMBER 1982–SEPTEMBER 1989

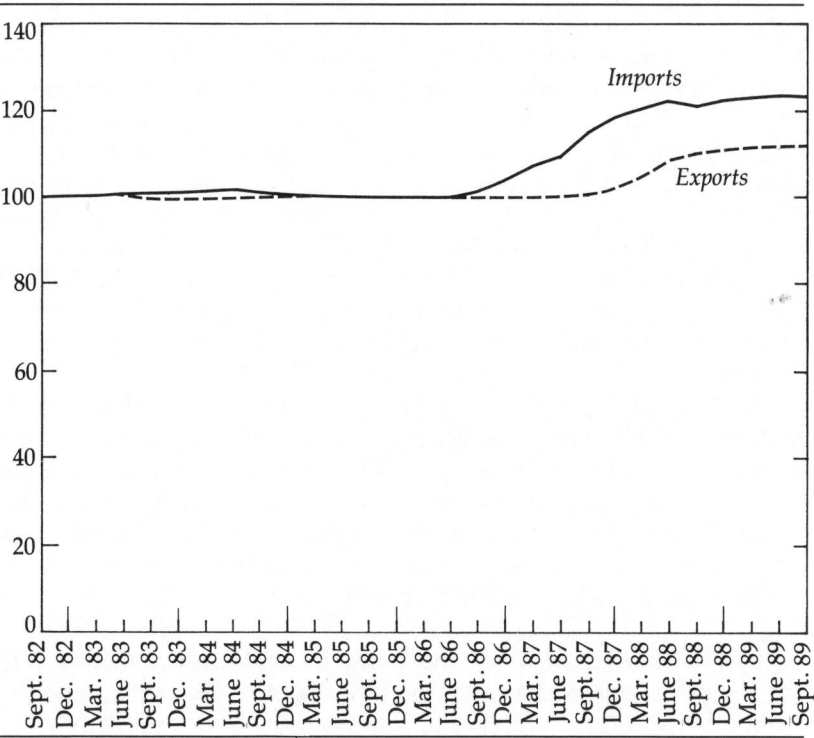

SOURCE: Bureau of Labor Statistics, U.S. Department of Labor.

labor-intensive import-competing goods fell relatively during the 1980s: without that, they cannot invoke the SS or the FPE variety of argumentation to "explain" the decline in unskilled-labor wages. In fact, there seems to be no evidence to suggest that the external terms of trade improved significantly in the 1980s for the United States, although this may have as much to do with the lack of exogenous improvement as to the increased adoption of voluntary export restraints that generally transfer rents to exporters and thus offset the improvement in terms of trade.

At minimum, as noted by Bhagwati (1991a), if one looks at the import and export price indexes for manufactured goods (which exceed 90 percent in weight in the total indexes) in figure 2–3, the evidence points the other way: import prices *rise* relative to export

51

prices.[21] A subsequent empirical study by Lawrence and Slaughter (1993) has reinforced the Bhagwati critique. The authors find a rise in the relative price of nonproduction-labor (skilled labor)-intensive goods as against production-labor (unskilled labor)-intensive goods at the 2- and 3-digit SIC classification levels. This more disaggregated analysis confirms the impression that our highly aggregated figure 2–3 conveys, since both show that the relative prices have moved in the "wrong" direction as far as the FPE-SS explanation is concerned.

A further critical piece of evidence presented by Lawrence and Slaughter is that most sectors (again, at the 2- and 3-digit levels) have become *more* intensive in their use of nonproduction labor as compared with production labor in the 1980s. This fact is at variance with the FPE-SS approach, since a key implication of the FPE-SS hypothesis is that firms in all sectors will economize on the more expensive factor, skilled labor, and hence will become more intensive in their use of unskilled labor.

This second piece of evidence, in conjunction with the first, effectively kills the FPE-SS hypothesis as a tenable explanation of the phenomenon of the rising wage differential and falling wages of the unskilled. The Borjas-Freeman-Katz conclusion that trade has adversely affected wages may well be right; but their analysis does not show this, and we can be quite confident that the FPE-SS explanation has been a red herring in the story.[22]

Technical Change—A Trade-Independent Explanation. Contrary to the Borjas-Freeman-Katz conclusion, both casual empiricism and the work of Mincer (1991), Davis and Haltiwanger (1991), and Bound and Johnson (1992) suggest strongly that skills-based technical change is the key culprit in the 1980s story and in the unfolding scenario for the 1990s and beyond.[23]

---

21. See Bhagwati (1991a) (1991b).

22. It is worth noting that several partial-equilibrium studies of the effect of trade on wages, which unlike Borjas-Freeman-Katz do use prices rather than quantities, most notably Grossman (1986, 1987) and Revenga (1992), also fail to find a significant effect of trade on wages in most of the industries studied.

23. The decline of unions, as discussed by Freeman (1991), the erosion of the real value of the minimum wage, as discussed in Blackburn, Bloom, and Freeman (1990), and changes in pay norms, as discussed by Mitchell (1989) are factors that, if taken into account, would imply that the pressure on real wages has been institutionally allowed to translate into actual decline in them. In the different, more "sheltering" type of EC institutional setting, conversely, this pressure presumably causes relatively less decline in wages

These labor economists cite the prototypical example of the computer revolution, a whole spectrum of technological innovations that inherently require their users to have skills easier for a college graduate than for a high school graduate to acquire today. To put it another way, a computer with a single skilled operator can replace half a dozen unskilled typists—a phenomenon that we see in our own departmental offices and in the publishing houses that bring out our books. In fact, the work of Mincer (1991) is extremely suggestive in this regard. Looking at research and development expenditures per worker, figure 2–4, panel A, and deploying a simple model, he is able to predict remarkably well (figure 2–4, panel B) the college graduates' wage premiums over the wages of high school graduates.

If, as in the section below on aggregate production function, we consider an *aggregate* production function approach, we can see readily that unskilled-labor-saving technical change (in a two-factor framework with skilled and unskilled labor) will reduce the wage differential and can depress the real wage of unskilled labor if the factor-substitution effect of the technical change is outweighed by the total productivity effect.[24]

The analysis gets more complex when we disaggregate the economy, as in the trade-theoretic models, into two sectors with different factor intensities. The effect on the wage differential and the real wage of the unskilled will depend then on the total rate of change, how biased it is against unskilled labor, and its relative incidence in the two sectors.

Thus, if the change is uniformly spread in both sectors, and the economy remains diversified in the new equilibrium at the old goods- and factor-price ratios, the result will be to maintain the wage differential. The factor-price ratio corresponding to the goods-price ratio will not change after the uniform technical change, whether Hicks-neutral or biased.[25] Although the real wage of unskilled labor will surely rise with Hicks-neutral technical change, it may not if the technical change is (pro-)skills-biased, and the bias effect outweighs the total productivity effect.

---

and more increase in unemployment. For a recent comprehensive survey of alternative explanations, see Levy and Murnane (1992).

24. Diagrammatically, the latter relates to the upward rescaling of the isoquants, whereas the former concerns their being twisted so that, at any factor-price ratio, the ratio of skilled to unskilled labor chosen rises as is consistent with the evidence (see the FPE section above).

25. The goods-price ratio can itself change if the country's terms of trade are variable: demand conditions then would have to be considered as well to determine the new equilibrium goods- and hence factor-price ratios.

FIGURE 2–4
WAGE PREMIUMS OF COLLEGE GRADUATES RELATIVE TO HIGH SCHOOL GRADUATES, WITH RESPECT TO R&D EXPENDITURES PER WORKER, 1963–1987

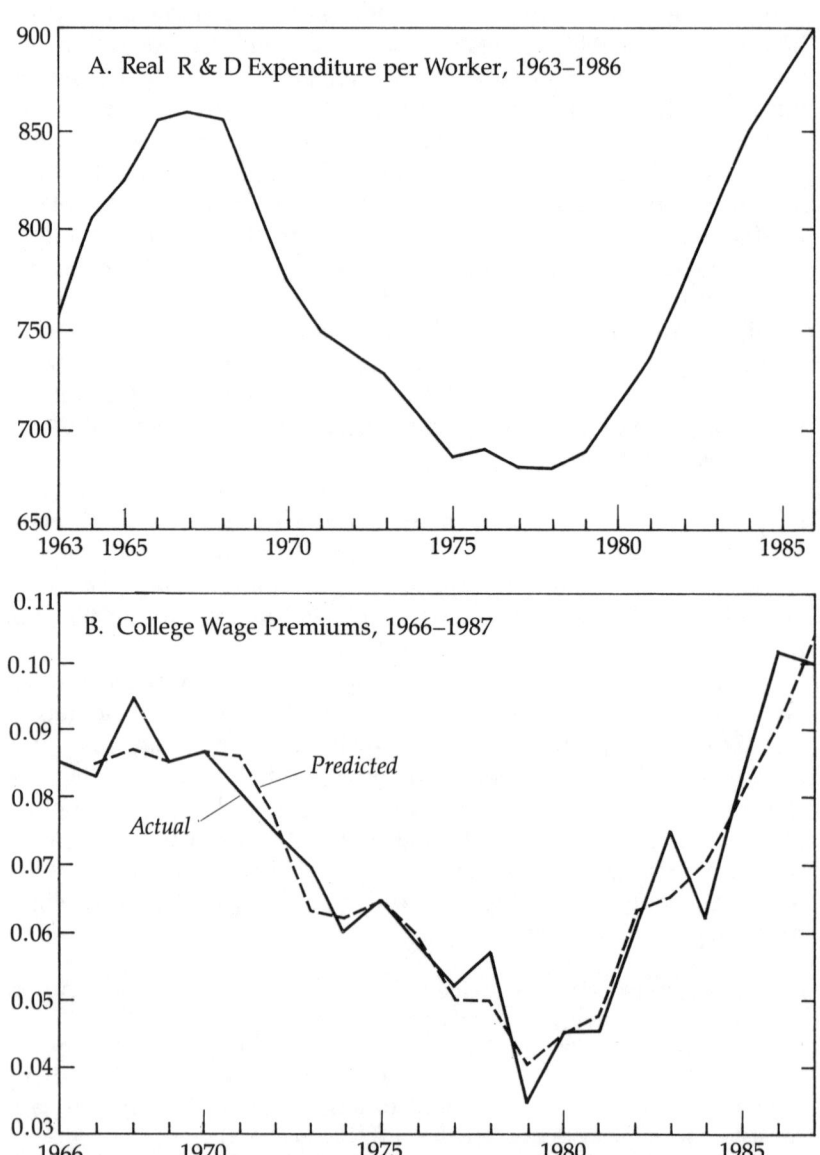

SOURCE: Jacob Mincer, *Studies in Human Capital: Collected Essays of Jacob Mincer,* vol. 1. Hampshire, England: Edward Elgar, 1993.

We would then argue that the disaggregated-sectors model suggests that the happy experience of the 1950s and 1960s may have been due to technical change that was substantial, was more uniformly spread among exportables and importables, and was more neutral than biased whereas, in the 1980s, it has probably been slower (perhaps due to slowed investment and hence slower absorption of new technology), has been more focused on skills-intensive exportables, and has been also more skills-biased. Taken in conjunction, these three factors would tend to widen the wage differential while putting downward pressure simultaneously on the real wages of the unskilled.[26] Of course, these ideas must be tested empirically.

But the preceding analysis takes technical change to be exogenous to trade. Larry Mishel has rightly raised the question: if trade competition *induces* technical change, could we not then relate the effects on real wages back again to trade? Our judgment, however, is that this would work against, not in favor of, those who think that trade is adversely affecting the real wages of the unskilled. For if we proceed along the assumption that trade competition induces neutral technical change in the import-competing unskilled-labor-intensive industries, this should raise, not lower, the real wage of the unskilled. Again, if we assume instead that trade exerts a little downward pressure on the real wages of the unskilled and that the search for technical innovation is biased in favor of economizing the use of the factors of production whose wages are rising instead, the effect again will be to reinforce the conclusion that trade-induced technical change helps, not hurts, the real wages of the unskilled.[27]

Kaleidoscopic Comparative Advantage—Footloose Industries and Labor Turnover

The technical-change-based explanation, of course, takes us away from trade as a cause of the phenomenon of depressed real wages of the unskilled. Indeed, it was the difficulty we had with the FPE-cum-SS-theoretic approach to this conundrum that helped focus on this alternative explanation.

But if the obvious FPE-SS-type trade explanation is not compelling, all is not lost. It is possible to develop an alternative trade-based

---

26. These ideas were explored in the context of a general-equilibrium model of two tradeable goods and two factors plus a nontrades services sector, using the Komiya model, in Bhagwati (1991a) (1991b).

27. See the discussion of the Kennedy-Weizsacker theory of induced technical change in Samuelson (1965).

explanation (Bhagwati 1991a; 1991b) that departs altogether from the FPE-SS approach. We doubt that this alternative explanation can carry the weight that the technical-change (and technological) explanation probably does, but it could well be a contributory factor of some, perhaps also growing, importance.

The new hypothesis comes from the observation that the world economy is now increasingly integrated and that the convergence of technology among the Organization for Economic Cooperation and Development (OECD) countries and the spread of global multinational corporations around the world have brought many modern industries within the grasp of countries. Many more industries therefore are "footloose" now than before: small shifts in costs can cause comparative advantage to shift suddenly from one country to another.[28] Thus, we suspect that comparative advantage has, over time, become kaleidoscopic: one country may have comparative advantage in X and another in Y today, and tomorrow it may suddenly go the other way. This volatility in comparative advantage will have two serious consequences.

The first consequence will be far greater sensitivity to notions of fair trade. Firms will be looking over one another's shoulders to see if that lethal epsilon advantage enjoyed by the other firm is attributable to some unfair domestic institution or policy on its home turf. Demands for "level playing fields" will multiply. They have already done so, as we noted in the first section of this chapter.

The second consequence is that the volatility in comparative advantage will generally imply, *ceteris paribus*, more labor turnover. Thus the frictional or "natural" unemployment should rise, as it appears to have in the 1980s. But the added turnover, in turn, could mean that the growth curve of earnings may become flatter, because a more mobile labor force could be accumulating less skills. As one of the authors, Bhagwati, has written elsewhere (Bhagwati 1991a and 1991b), "a rolling stone gathers no moss and a moving worker gathers no skills." As it happens, a forthcoming study by the OECD, reported on by *The Economist* (1993) in the Economics Focus column entitled "Musical Chairs," confirms this conjecture:

> So the OECD concludes that there is a clear link between employment stability and skill training. But which causes which? Most likely the two are mutually reinforcing: too

---

28. This is also the view implicit in the imperfect-competition worlds of symmetric firms, although the analysis often goes in the direction of arguing how footloose industries land in one rather than another country as scale economies are exploited.

high a rate of labor turnover discourages investment in work-place skills; and workers who get no training are likely to show less commitment to their current employer and so may change jobs more often. A vicious circle develops as higher labor turnover produces a less trained and hence a less loyal workforce.

Then, we get a trade-dependent explanation as to why increased labor turnover reduces, *ceteris paribus*, the real wage of unskilled labor. But what about the wage *differential* between unskilled and skilled labor? Our argument seems to apply symmetrically to all labor. Therefore, to produce an explanation of increased wage differential as well, we would have to introduce some source of asymmetry that relatively shields the skilled from the rolling-stone-gathers-no-moss effect.

Such an asymmetry may accrue from the greater transferability of workplace-acquired skills by the skilled. An accountant handling IBM, for example, can shift his acquired knowhow readily to a new job at Caterpillar or Chrysler, but working better on the assembly line for autos at Ford may not transfer to working at a blast furnace in Pittsburgh, or for that matter to flipping hamburgers at MacDonalds.

Again, the fallow, search-period spells between jobs are probably used by college graduates (the skilled) to retool and acquire added and more suitable skills—having learned once, one can and will learn again. High school graduates and dropouts (the unskilled) are less likely to do so, having not learned in the first place. We can only speculate about this; empirical knowledge is hard to come by on this particular hypothesis. Jacob Mincer and Yoshio Higuchi's 1988 study attempts to link labor turnover and the wage structure. Although it does not directly address the hypothesis we have advanced, this study could provide the basis for its empirical investigation. Furthermore, Steve Davis has suggested that one useful empirical construct that could be brought to bear on the hypothesis is the tenure distribution in various disaggregated sectors of the economy. If sectors that were exposed to the rolling-stone-gathers-no-moss effect of the type discussed here also exhibited leftward shifts in the tenure distributions, especially of unskilled workers, then this would be consistent with the hypothesis and might constitute partial corroboration of it.

A Rolling-Stone-Gathers-No-Moss Model. We can readily sketch the essential structure of the foregoing argument in the 2×2 framework.[29] Let the economy be small—that is, the terms of trade are

---

29. See also Dehejia (1992b). The model is set up to generate not merely the adverse effect on the real wage of the unskilled, but also a widening

given and invariant to its trade. Let two goods, X and Y, be produced according to standard neoclassical production functions with the use of two factors, skilled labor, H, and unskilled labor, L, which throughout are in fixed supply. Suppose as well that the terms of trade are such that this economy exports good X and that the economy remains within the Chipman-McKenzie diversification cone.

To capture the notion of volatility in terms of trade, suppose a two-period structure in which the terms of trade of the skilled-labor-intensive good initially improve but then return to their original level. That is, suppose that the initial relative price of good X in terms of good Y is p, then it becomes p', $p'>p$, and finally returns to p.[30]

As regards the accumulation of human capital, this for simplicity is assumed to take place between periods—that is, between the period in which terms of trade p' and p prevail. Suppose that both types of labor, skilled and unskilled, acquire human capital through learning-by-doing, which is modeled as an augmentation of the effective stocks of the two types of labor, H and L. Crucially, skilled labor, H, augments at the same rate in either sector, X or Y. This augmentation is assumed to be unaffected by a shift of skilled labor between sectors.

Therefore, suppose that H augments at the end of the two periods to δH, $\delta>1$, where δ is the gross rate of growth of the effective stock of H. By contrast, unskilled labor, L, augments if it remains in the same sector, but it is assumed not to augment if it moves between sectors. Therefore, total augmentation of the effective stock of unskilled labor, L, is $\delta(L-\Delta L)+\Delta L$, where ΔL is the amount of unskilled labor that moves between sectors X and Y in response to the initial terms of trade shift from p to p'.

This is illustrated in figure 2–5 with the aid of the family Edgeworth-Bowley box diagram. Let $OPP'O'$ be the contract curve. At the initial terms of trade, the economy is at point P on $OPP'O'$. The change in trade from p to p' induces a shift in the equilibrium to a

---

differential between the wages of the unskilled and the skilled. While we use the words "skilled" and "unskilled," Alan Deardorff has correctly noted that, since both types of labor can acquire skills but only differentially as assumed, it would be better to think of college and high school graduates, as earlier in this chapter.

30. In more general form, we can envisage a stochastic progress for the terms of trade in which there are stationary disturbances around some trend growth rate (which may be zero, in which case the terms of trade would be pure white noise). See also Dehejia (1992b).

FIGURE 2–5
REALLOCATION OF LABOR IN RESPONSE TO TERMS OF TRADE SHOCK

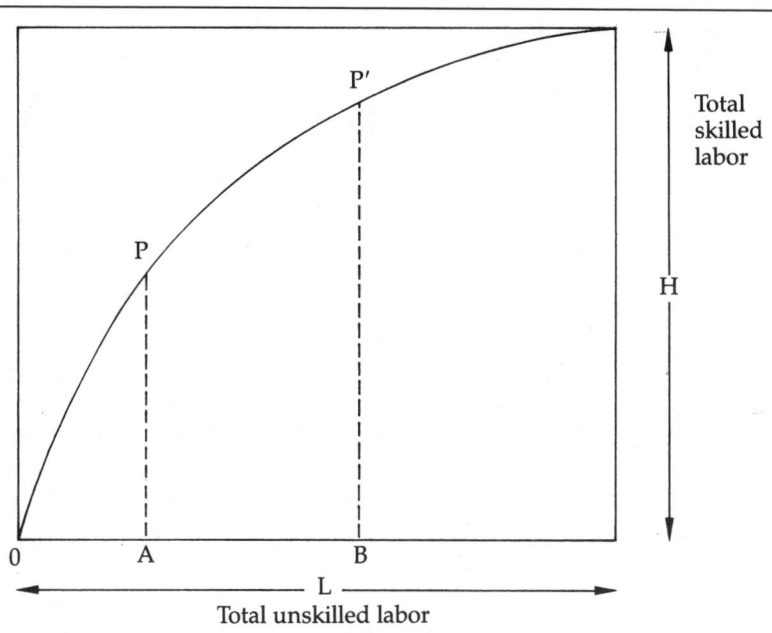

SOURCE: Authors.

new point, P', along $OPP'O'$. Drop vertical lines from P and P' to the horizontal axis and label the corresponding points A and B, respectively. Then ΔL is equal to the distance AB along the horizontal axis.

In the final equilibrium, when the terms of trade have returned to p, there is no change in the real wage per effective unit of skilled or unskilled labor. The effective stocks per worker of the two factors now differ, however, because of differential augmentation induced by the fluctuation of p to p' before its return to p. The effective stock of skilled labor is now δH, whereas the effective stock of unskilled labor is now $\delta(L-\Delta L) + \Delta L$.[31] This differential augmentation induces a

31. This model assumes that real wages will adjust immediately and fully to terms of trade changes. But in reality there are often lags. Besides, if one thinks of models of labor hiring and firing, their microeconomics suggests that, if terms of trade are expected to be volatile, firms will not adjust their employment to every change in the price of their output. Models that incorporate these ideas should nonetheless show that increased volatility of goods prices will be associated with increased volatility of factor prices.

Rybczynski (1955)-type reallocation of resources from the unskilled labor-intensive sector, Y, to the skilled labor-intensive sector, X, but with no effect on the real wage per effective worker of either type, since diversification is assumed.

Although real wages per effective worker are unchanged, however, the observed real wages per worker now differ. Recall that H and L represent total effective stocks of skilled and unskilled labor, respectively. Normalizing the populations of skilled and unskilled labor to unity for simplicity, H and L may thus be interpreted as the total stock of skilled labor per skilled laborer and the total stock of unskilled labor per unskilled laborer, respectively. Initially, the real wage of a skilled worker is $W_H H$ and that of an unskilled worker $W_L L$, where W_H and W_L are the respective real wages per effective worker.

At the end, real wages per effective worker, W_H and W_L, are unchanged, but real wages per worker have increased to $W_H \delta H$ and $W_L(\delta[L\text{-}\Delta L] + \Delta L)$, respectively.

Thus, while real wages per worker of both skilled and unskilled labor have increased because of on-the-job human capital accumulation, skilled labor becomes relatively better off (as compared with the initial situation) than unskilled labor. The real income of unskilled labor will thus be lower, as compared with having no terms of trade volatility in this model. This is caused not by the SS effect on real wages, as discussed in the FPE section above, but by the differential human capital accumulation that leaves unskilled labor relatively poorly endowed with human capital at the end. Skilled labor, conversely, by the model's assumption is impervious to the volatility in terms of trade. It is evident that the real wage per unskilled laborer will be lower than if the rolling-stone effect were absent.

A multiperiod version of this model has been analyzed by Dehejia (1992b), combining the analytics of the 2×2 model of trade theory with the twin new assumptions of the rolling-stone hypothesis on skills acquisition. The terms of trade of this small country evolve according to a pure, white-noise stochastic process. The terms of trade are assumed to have no trend, but rather to fluctuate noisily around some unspecified, long-run level, attributable to unspecified worldwide technology or taste shocks.

The simulation runs of the wage differentials (per worker)[32] that the model then generates, per our hypothesis attributable to the

---

32. The wages per effective worker (that is, for given skill) remain constant in expected value terms by model specification of stationary white noise disturbances to the terms of trade. The trend change in a worker's real wage can come only from the acquisition of more skills in this model.

terms of trade fluctuations and the induced divergence of skills acquisition between the skilled and unskilled workers, do indeed show a rising time trend. Simulation runs by Dehejia on different values of the terms of trade noise parameter bear out the intuitive notion that the higher this parameter and hence the greater the volatility in terms of trade, the larger the wage-differential effect that is generated.[33]

Hysteresis—An Alternative Link between Kaleidoscopic Comparative Advantage and Wages. The modeling hitherto cited has simply embodied, in the otherwise-static framework, the rolling-stone-gathers-no-moss idea. There were no supply-side effects, in that each of the two types of labor followed its own skills-acquisition trajectory, as influenced critically by the kaleidoscopic-comparative-advantage-implied volatility in the terms of trade.

But, of course, the two groups are not predetermined and nonintersecting over time. The unskilled (high school graduates and dropouts) can and do become skilled (college graduates and more) if the rewards are enticing. In the foregoing model, if the unskilled could costlessly become skilled, the relative supply of skilled labor would be infinitely elastic at a zero differential: that is, any wage differential induced by terms of trade shifts would instantaneously disappear, which obviously is unrealistic.

But, to allow for costly fixed investment to enter the skilled group, we can realistically explore further the wage-differential and wage effect of volatility in terms of trade. To do this, we must obviously introduce hysteresis into the analysis.[34] We now indicate how this might be done.

Take again as our starting point increased volatility in terms of trade, and introduce Dixit-style hysteresis in the following simple way. Thus, suppose that unskilled workers can transform themselves into skilled workers by incurring an irreversible fixed cost K.[35] Suppose next that the relative reward to being skilled versus being

---

33. For details, see Dehejia (1992b). The simulations are necessary because an analytical solution to the model is not possible because of the inherent nonlinearity in the key equation defining the time path of effective skilled-to-unskilled labor in the model.

34. For a recent survey and synthesis of results in the investment and hysteresis literature, see Dixit (1992), on which we draw below.

35. Formally, we must assume for analytical tractability in this simple model that the skilled can costlessly become unskilled. For professors who see how rapidly most students forget a subject once the examinations are over, this may well be the most realistic assumption in this chapter.

unskilled fluctuates stochastically (because of fluctuations in terms of trade) according to a geometric Brownian motion process (the continuous time analog of the random walk in discrete time). Under the critical assumption of a fixed cost of investment in an environment characterized by ongoing uncertainty, a band of inaction or hysteresis region will exist in which the wage differential (the excess return to being skilled versus being unskilled) will be positive, and in which there will be no supply response by unskilled workers to eliminate this differential.

It is important to note that hysteresis per se arises because of the existence of linear adjustment technology (that is, a fixed cost of retraining per worker), as opposed to neoclassical convex adjustment technology. Even in the absence of uncertainty, an inaction region will exist in which no retraining will take place. In a world without uncertainty, retraining will occur at the Marshallian investment trigger M, where M is defined by:

$$M = \rho K,$$

where ρ is individuals' pure rate of time preference, which we can assume equals the interest rate. By assumption of the model, sufficient retraining will occur when the trigger is reached to ensure that the wage differential will never exceed ρK. Thus, for example, if it costs $100,000 for an unskilled worker to "upskill," so that $K = 100,000$, and if the interest rate is equal to 5 percent, so that $\rho = 0.05$, then the maximum sustainable wage differential, which is equal to the Marshallian investment trigger M, is given by $(.05 \times 100,000)$, or $5,000. The skilled job thus must pay $5,000 more than the unskilled job to elicit a supply response. Furthermore, in this simple model that is the maximum differential consistent with labor market equilibrium.[36]

The effect of uncertainty is essentially to *widen* the hysteresis region by increasing the investment trigger from M, given above, to H, where:

$$H = \rho' K,$$

where the interest rate ρ must be replaced by an adjusted interest rate ρ', where $\rho' > \rho$. The precise definition of ρ' is furnished in Dixit (1992). It suffices for our purposes here to notice that the existence of uncertainty can make ρ' exceed ρ by an amount that is not trivial. Thus, sticking to the example in which $\rho = 0.05$, if we assume that σ, the coefficient of variation of the Brownian motion, is 0.2—a magni-

---

36. For details see Dixit (1992).

tude of uncertainty by no means large, since the standard deviation is 20 percent of the mean of the distribution—then ρ' is shown by Dixit to equal 0.093, or 9.3 percent, giving a maximum wage differential of $9,300.

Intuitively, in an inherently uncertain economic environment in which investment is costly and irreversible, in the sense that once an unskilled worker spends K to upskill he can never recover the investment, an unskilled worker will be reluctant to upskill because there is always the danger that the skill differential will drop after the costly investment is made. Of course, even in the presence of uncertainty, given a big enough wage differential, an unskilled worker will still be willing to upskill.

The existence of uncertainty essentially attaches a risk premium to the investment decision to upskill, which will raise the "hurdle rate" on the investment. Furthermore, it is intuitively appealing (and is proved rigorously by Dixit) that this risk premium increases with the magnitude of uncertainty. Thus, in the numerical example above, if ρ remains at 5 percent but σ is now set to 0.4, then ρ' jumps to 0.166, or 16.6 percent—a very high hurdle rate indeed—which raises the maximum skill differential that the labor market will sustain to $16,600.

The connection between the Dixit-type hysteresis model and the assumption of terms of trade volatility made in this section thus becomes apparent. If indeed our assumption is correct that the 1980s have witnessed increased volatility in trade and hence induced volatility in the relative-demand-driven wage differential, then the model suggests that in this increasingly uncertain economic environment, unskilled workers become increasingly reluctant to upskill. Hence, wage differentials that are larger than the historical norm will likely be observed.

Thus consider for illustration figure 2–6. Let H_0 be the investment trigger corresponding to an initial low level of uncertainty before the 1980s (σ_0), and let $H_1 > H_0$ be the new, higher investment trigger corresponding to a new, higher level of uncertainty in the 1980s (σ_1). Then the wage differential, which fluctuates stochastically in the smaller inaction band before the 1980s, breaks through its historical ceiling at date t', and rises above H_0, since now the new trigger level H_1 is applicable. It is not until date t'' that the wage differential reaches its new ceiling, given by H_1, after which it cannot perforce rise any more. Thus, if t' is, say, 1980, and t'' is some indeterminate date in the future, then the time interval $[t', t'']$ would be characterized by a rising wage differential. This would seem puzzling to those accustomed to H_0 as the old maximum wage differential, presumably

FIGURE 2–6

LARGER WAGE DIFFERENTIAL INDUCED BY GREATER VOLATILITY OF TERMS
OF TRADE

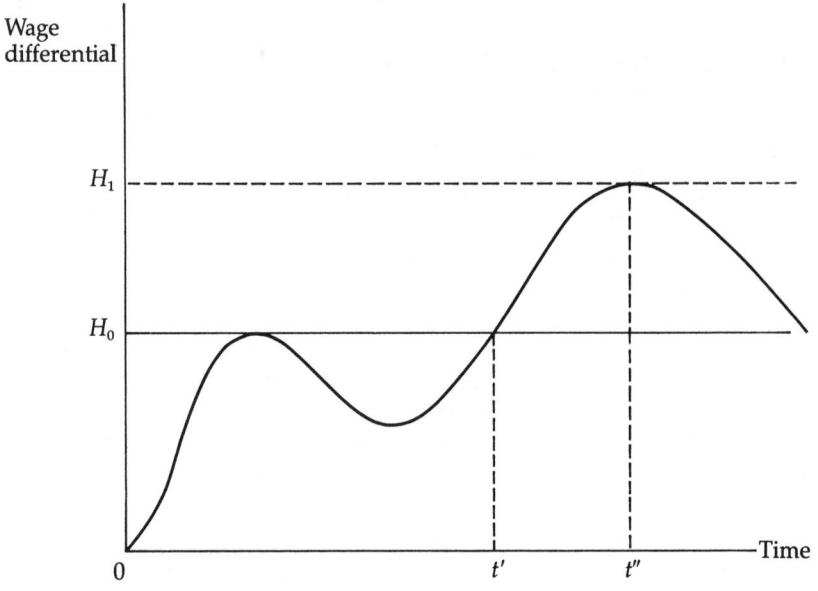

SOURCE: Authors.

thought of as the historical norm, if H_0 had persisted for a long
enough time. It makes sense, however, once it is understood that the
level of uncertainty has increased.

Not only does this simple model build on the assumption of
kaleidoscopic comparative advantage, and hence volatility of terms of
trade, as did the rolling-stone model above; it is also ground firmly in
individual choice–theoretic terms. This is its strength, and it helps to
explain the puzzle first noted, it seems, by Jacob Mincer that the
1980s and early 1990s witnessed wage differentials well above historical norms. Relative supply responses have been muted compared
with previous episodes of relatively high wage differentials.

An important corollary follows from this model. Since the action
points are individually optimal in this model, and since, in the
absence of any distortions in the system, those points are therefore
also the social action points, it follows that the bigger wage differentials observed in periods of higher uncertainty are also socially optimal. This corollary holds provided that such increased uncertainty is

treated as truly exogenous and produced by kaleidoscopic comparative advantage in a highly globalized economy today.

In other words, in an inherently more uncertain environment, unskilled workers are doing the smart thing in delaying their decision to upskill. Hence the big wage differential we observe today should not be of policy concern. Government policy to narrow the differential by, say, subsidizing retraining by unskilled workers would be harmful in that some unskilled workers would be induced by the government subsidy scheme to retrain whereas they had previously optimally chosen to remain unskilled. The increment to their income gained from upskilling would not be large enough to warrant the investment.

Legitimate policy concerns about the incomes of the unskilled should therefore be met not by implementing retraining schemes but by direct *lump sum* income transfers to them. These transfers would accomplish the income distributional goals of policy without distorting incentives pertaining to the upskilling investment decision.

This conclusion, of course, presumes that the reduced real wages of the unskilled produced by other factors (such as the rolling-stone effect) have not produced an imperfection in the credit market for borrowing to educate oneself. The effect of such a distortion in the context of the previous model is effectively to increase the private hurdle rate to some $\rho'' > \rho'$, whereas the social hurdle rate remains ρ'. The emergence of such distortions in the 1980s would provide an independent argument for subsidizing training and education to high school graduate and dropouts, the objective being to subsidize the unskilled workers to the extent that the gap ($\rho'' - \rho'$) is eliminated.

Trade and Rents

We now turn to a more conventional, trade-related explanation that builds on the incorporation of imperfectly competitive *factor* markets into the picture. It is often claimed that international competition has led to the erosion of high-wage jobs, especially for autos and steel: either they have disappeared, or the wages on such "good" jobs have been scaled down.

In the sense that the decline in the product prices of these sectors is putting downward pressure on labor that is specific to them or is intensively used in them, the resulting decline in the real wage of such labor is simply the SS phenomenon. But the aforementioned argument is rather that identical-quality labor is getting a higher wage (and hence a rent) in the import-competing sectors and that this rent will be reduced in the new equilibrium, or that the number of people enjoying unchanged rents (that is, the number of good jobs) will be reduced, thanks to the import competition (that is, improved terms of trade).

Two questions must be asked before we consider this argument analytically: (1) is there any evidence that there are such rents? and (2) why do these rents exist?

The chief source of the current acceptance of the importance of rents in labor markets is the empirical work of Katz and Summers (1989) for U.S. industries for 1984. They estimate the interindustry dispersion of wages, controlling them for explanatory variables but finding that the standard deviation of the estimated wage differentials falls from 28 percent without these controls to 15 percent with them. This leaves a residual, which is then assigned to rents. The recent work of Jacob Mincer (1993), however, by adding better estimates of training and other variables and using different data sets, has succeeded in wiping out more than half of the Katz-Summers residual, leaving too emasculated a result to base serious explanations and policy conclusions on.[37]

But assuming that the rents were significant, what could have caused them? The obvious answer is that the rents are obtained and protected by trade unions. This is surely true for the two major tradeable sectors that have faced import competition: autos and steel. In the more diffused analysis that Katz and Summers deploy, extended to aggregated groups of industries in the United States, accounting for unions nonetheless leaves a residual to be explained by other factors. Katz and Summers then opt for an efficiency wage explanation of the type produced by Leibenstein and Mirrlees many years ago via the productivity effects of higher wages from better nourishment in developing countries and now extended to developed countries, in the shape of raising the cost of being fired and hence increasing efficiency in jobs where shirking is possible. As far as we can tell, Katz and Summers do not explore the technology of the industries where they do find significant nonunion-related rents to see if the hypothesis of shirking makes sense. It would appear that in sectors such as services, where one might be working on one's own in relation to customers, shirking is easier than in manufacturing, where shirking may be difficult because of being on a tight assembly line with many others. Yet the rents seem to be higher in the latter than in the former. Then again, the rents seem to obtain in all jobs in an industry rather than in specific jobs in it; but it is hard

---

37. This is not to say that the efficiency-wage models are not of great intellectual interest. Their relevance to the issue at hand is what we doubt.

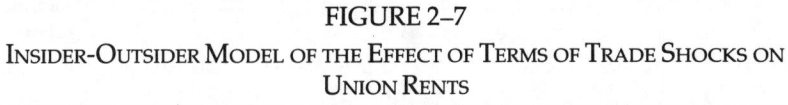

FIGURE 2–7

INSIDER-OUTSIDER MODEL OF THE EFFECT OF TERMS OF TRADE SHOCKS ON
UNION RENTS

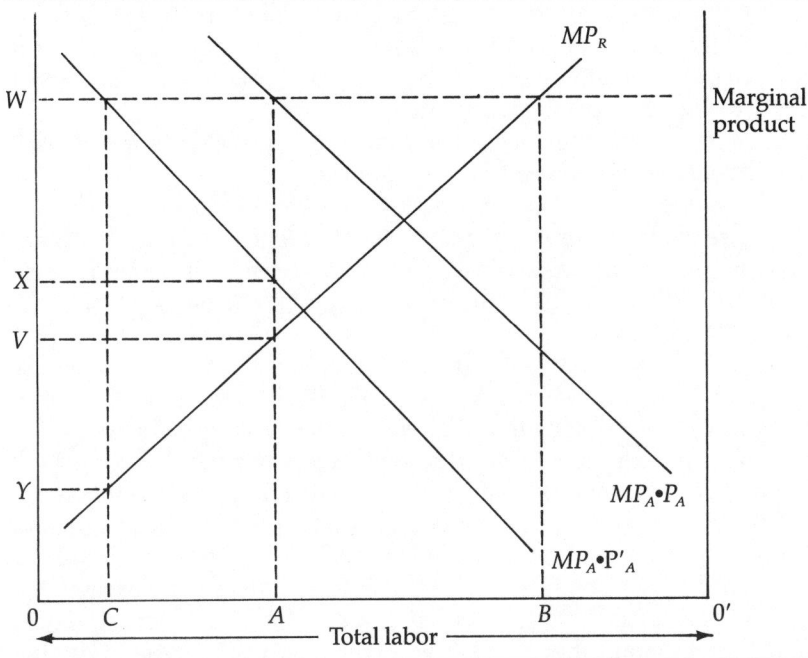

SOURCE: Authors.

to see why technology should be such that shirking obtains for all operations in an industry. Then again, Jacob Mincer's work shows that the average time spent in a queue for the higher-wage jobs is not longer than elsewhere, suggesting that the higher wages are for better people, whereas the "rent" explanation would suggest longer wait-time instead.

For these reasons, we do not pursue the idea of modeling here the effect of import competition on rents in efficiency-wage models. Besides, a scanning of the Katz-Summers findings by industry does not suggest any relationship between rents in an industry and its status as a nontradeable or tradeable and, if tradeable, as an exportable or an importable. We therefore confine ourselves to modeling the effect of import competition—that is, of fall in world prices on trade-union–generated rents and jobs.

Consider then a simple general-equilibrium insider-outsider model, as in figure 2–7. Suppose that the economy consists of two

67

sectors: A, autos, and R, the rest. Suppose that the workers in sector R are competitive, whereas the auto workers are controlled by a union.[38] Suppose further that the union insiders are OA in number. OO' is the total labor force. P_A is the relative price of autos, and MPs are the marginal product curves, measured for R from O' and for A from O as the origins. With OA insiders, whose full employment it will ensure, the auto union will then bargain for (and we assume that the firms will accept) the wage rate OW.

There are at least three ways to close the model in terms of labor market behavior in the rest of the economy:

First, we can assume that the union-determined wage has such widespread appeal that it perhaps becomes legislated into an economy-wide minimum wage of OW. In that case, employment in the rest of the economy will be $O'B$, and unemployment of magnitude AB will be observed.

Second, we can assume that the wage in the rest of the economy falls sufficiently to ensure economy-wide full employment. In that case, wage OV will obtain in the rest of the economy, which is lower by VW than the union wage in that auto sector, and AO' workers will be employed in the rest of the economy, with no unemployment.

Third, there may be a convex combination of the first and second alternatives, in that wages in the rest of the economy may be below OW but not far enough below to eliminate all unemployment. A version of this third hypothesis is essentially the Harris-Todaro model from development theory.[39] We will work with the second hypothesis, since that is consistent with the wage differentials observed by Katz and Summers (1989) and does not involve unemployment, which is not central to the current discussion and would only complicate matters unnecessarily.

Now, to tell the "rent-squeezing" story, suppose a deterioration in terms of trade for autos vis-à-vis other goods. This implies an inward shift of the marginal product of labor schedule, MP_A, in proportion to the terms of trade change. If this change is anticipated by insiders, they will bargain for wage OX, which ensures full employment by insiders. Nominal wage will fall to OX, but notice that the real wage denominated in autos has remained constant, since nominal wages fall in proportion to the fall in terms of trade. Since by construction the numeraire is all other goods, the real wage will have fallen in terms of all other goods. Thus, insider autoworkers

---

38. We make no Freudian slip in using the word "controlled." Substitute the word "represented" if desired.

39. Compare Harris and Todaro (1970) and Bhagwati and Srinivasan (1974).

will typically perceive a fall in their real wages (unless they consume only autos for breakfast instead of corn flakes), but insider employment will be protected.[40]

Consider an alternative scenario in which the fall in trade was unexpected by the union. Then the union will bargain for and receive wage OW, but labor demand will fall short of MP_A. Thus the number of insiders will shrink to OC, with the disenfranchised insiders joining low-paid workers in the rest of the economy and earning the low wage OY. Now, what has happened to real wages? Since the nominal wage did not change, the real wage in terms of autos goes up (since the price of autos went down). Since other goods are our numeraire, the real wage in terms of other goods stays constant. Thus, the real wage for the few insiders who are still employed will rise or stay roughly constant, but it will not fall. Good jobs will shrink, becoming even better jobs, and bad jobs will increase.

The two stories above at a very crude level might seem to fit the stylized facts of the United States and European Community respectively. In the United States, wages appear to be flexible downward, and thus insider employment levels in autos and steel are essentially unchanged. In the European Community, by contrast, wages have been rigid and employment in autos and steel has been falling. If this simple insider-outsider model is correct, then either the U.S. unions expected the shock and thus bargained for lower wages and European unions did not, or (stepping beyond the model) European unions stuck fast for high wages, as they were presumably concerned about the "superinsiders" OC, whereas U.S. unions cared about OA and thus let wages fall.[41]

Aggregate Production Function—The Ultimate Threat?

The models deployed in the foregoing analysis have been disaggregated (at least two sectors, exportables and importables) and in general equilibrium. But suppose we examine an aggregate production function for the entire economy.

This makes it analytically impossible to consider trade questions

---

40. The real wage of R-workers will rise, however, because of cheaper autos, thus diluting the *total* reduction in the real wage of workers.

41. Thea Lee has suggested that the effect of trade competition may simply be to weaken the unions' bargaining power generally. Thus, a shift from protecting insiders' wages to protecting their employment may soon yield to inability to be taken seriously and hence their eventual demise. If so, rents defining some jobs as better than other jobs will obviously vanish with the unions.

meaningfully. But it is perfectly compatible with thinking about the effects of accumulation and of technical change. [The real problem with it is that it can be quite misleading, since disaggregation shows, as trade theorists are aware, that effects such as diminishing returns, which seem natural and inevitable in the context of aggregate production functions, can be eliminated by compositional effects. Thus, for example, if David Card's (1990) findings on the failure of the Mariel influx of Cubans into Miami are correct, and there was no effect of the substantial influx on real wages in Miami, that may well be because, as the Rybczynski (1955) theorem underlines, the added labor may have been absorbed at constant goods and factor prices by relative expansion of labor-intensive activities: a hypothesis that we suspect has not been examined.]

Using then the aggregate production function approach, suppose that we allow explicitly for three factors: capital K, skilled labor L_S, and unskilled labor L_U. Then take a nested *CES* production function that captures the idea that K and L_S are relatively complementary, as compared with L_U.[42] In that case, the marginal product of L_U, and hence its real wage, will *fall* as capital accumulates. Technology is thus not kind to unskilled labor: the traditional engine for growth, Marx's primitive accumulation, hurts unskilled labor instead of improving its real wage. The same applies, of course, if we receive net inflows of foreign investment. Ross Perot gets to stand on his head!

Furthermore, technical change accentuates this phenomenon in the production function above,[43] as indeed in the real world, as the recent work on technical change confirms (for example, see Krueger [1993]). Then, we have a real problem on our hands: *both* sources of

---

42. Such a production function is:

$$Y = \{\delta[\alpha K^{-\rho 1} + (1 - \alpha)L_S^{-\rho 1}]^{\rho 2/\rho 1} + (1 - \delta)L_U^{-\rho 2}\}^{-1/\rho 2},$$

where the condition that $\rho 1 > \rho 2$ guarantees that capital K and skilled labor L_S have a lower Hicks-Allen partial substitution elasticity than K and unskilled labor L_U, so that capital-skill complementarity holds in a relative sense. The production function is from Layard and Walters (1978). The original work on the three-factor production function, with the thesis that capital is more complementary with skilled labor, is due to Griliches (1969). More recent evidence is presented in Bartel and Lichtenberg (1987) and Berndt and Morrison (1991).

43. This is easily verified by multiplying the production function in the preceding footnote with a technology shift parameter A and then showing that the marginal product of unskilled labor (the partial derivative of Y with respect to L_U) is decreasing in A.

growth, capital accumulation (including inward foreign investment) and technical change, will harm unskilled labor. That becomes then the *ultimate threat*. Marx is indeed striking again.

Once again, the analysis exaggerates and misleads. Compositional effects can kill the operation of the adverse effect within each industry. Then again, supply response by the unskilled to get skilled as the returns to skills rise will reduce *ceteris paribus* the supply of unskilled labor and increase that of the skilled. This effect will make the widened differential in rewards to the skilled relative to the unskilled a transitory phenomenon. The adjustment process whereby the unskilled become skilled, turning the differential back toward its original position, depends of course on the cost of such skill acquisition.[44]

We may conjecture here, however, that the adjustment may have become more costly, and hence the widening of the wage differential more persistent, in the 1980s. This could have been caused by the rise of lucrative alternatives such as drug-dealing, the fall in the quality of schools, and the collapse of the family and hence the fall in the motivation and aptitude for getting educated among those affected, particularly in inner cities.

Concluding Remark

Our review and analysis of alternative *theoretical* ways in which freer trade may affect real wages of the unskilled suggest several areas for further investigation.

But they also indicate that the *empirical* evidence to date fails to put the burden of the explanation for the observed decline in real wages of the unskilled on freer trade, leaving technology and technical change as the key culprits.

---

44. The transition-path and the steady-state properties of such an adjustment process have been examined in Dehejia (1992a).

References

Bartel, Ann P., and Frank R. Lichtenberg. "The Comparative Advantage of Educated Workers in Implementing New Technology." *Review of Economics and Statistics*, vol. 69, 1987, pp. 343–59.

Baumol, William J., Sue Anne B. Blackman, and Edward N. Wolff. *Productivity and American Leadership: The Long View.* Cambridge, Mass.: MIT Press, 1989.

Berndt, Earnst R., and Catherine Morrison. "High-Tech Capital, Economic Performance, and Labor Composition in U.S. Manufacturing Industries: An Exploratory Analysis." Mimeo, Cambridge, Mass., MIT, 1991.

Bhagwati, Jagdish N. "Protection, Real Wages and Real Incomes." *Economic Journal*, vol. 69, pp. 733–48.

———. "The Pure Theory of International Trade: A Survey." *Economic Journal*, vol. 74, 1964, pp. 1–94.

———. "Free Traders and Free Immigrationists: Strangers or Friends?" Working Paper no. 20, Russell Sage Foundation, New York, N.Y., 1991 [1991a].

———. "Trade and Income Distribution." Paper presented at the Columbia University conference, "Deindustrialization." New York, N.Y., November 15–16, 1991 [1991b].

———. *The World Trading System at Risk*. Princeton, N.J.: Princeton University Press, 1991 [1991c].

———. "Fair Trade, Reciprocity, and Harmonization: The New Challenge to the Theory and Policy of Free Trade." Forthcoming, in A. Deardorff and R. Stern, eds., volume on GATT. Ann Arbor, Mich.: University of Michigan Press, 1994 [1992].

Bhagwati, Jagdish N., and T. N. Srinivasan. "On Reanalyzing the Harris-Todaro Model: Policy Rankings in the Case of Sector-Specific Sticky Wages." *American Economic Review*, vol. 64, 1974, pp. 502–8.

———. *Lectures on International Trade*. Cambridge, Mass.: MIT Press, 1983.

Blackburn, McKinley L., David E. Bloom, and Richard B. Freeman. "The Declining Economic Position of Less Skilled American Men." In G. Burtless, ed., *A Future of Lousy Jobs?: The Changing Structure of U.S. Wages*. Washington, D.C.: Brookings Institution, 1990, pp. 31–67.

———. "An Era of Falling Earnings and Rising Inequality?" *Brookings Review*, vol. 9, 1990, pp. 38–43.

Borjas, George J., Richard B. Freeman, and Lawrence F. Katz. "On the Labor Market Effects of Immigration and Trade." In G. Borjas and R. Freeman, eds., *The Economic Effects of Immigration in Source and Receiving Countries*. Chicago, Ill.: University of Chicago Press, 1992.

Bound, John, and George Johnson. "Changes in the Structure of Wages in the 1980s: An Evaluation of Alternative Explanations." *American Economic Review*, vol. 82, 1992, pp. 371–92.

Brown, Drusilla K., Alan V. Deardorff, and Robert M. Stern. "Protection and Real Wages: Old and New Trade Theories and Their Empirical Counterparts." Paper presented the CEPR/CESPRI conference, "New Trade Theories: A Look at the Empirical Evidence." Bocconi University, Milan, May 27–28, 1993.

Card, David. "The Impact of the Mariel Boatlift on the Miami Labor Market." *Industrial and Labor Relations Review*, vol. 43, no. 2, 1990, pp. 245–57.

Cline, William R. *The Future of World Trade in Textiles and Apparel.* Washington, D.C.: Institute for International Economics, 1990.

Davis, Steven J., and John Haltiwanger. "Wage Dispersion between and within U.S. Manufacturing Plants, 1963–86." *Brookings Papers on Economic Activity, Microeconomics.* The Brookings Institution, Washington, D.C., 1991, pp. 115–80.

Deardorff, Alan V., and Dalia Hakura. "Trade and Wages: What Are the Questions?" Chapter 3 in this volume.

Deardorff, Alan V., and Jon D. Haveman. "The Effects of U.S. Trade Laws on Poverty in America." Discussion paper no. 285. Institute of Public Policy Studies, Ann Arbor, Mich.: University of Michigan, 1991.

Deardorff, Alan V., and Robert W. Staiger. "An Interpretation of the Factor Content of Trade." *Journal of International Economics*, vol. 24, 1988, pp. 93–107.

Dehejia, Vivek H. "Capital-Skill Complementarity and Endogenous Wage Structure." Mimeo, New York, N.Y., Columbia University, 1992 [1992a].

———. "Kaleidoscopic Comparative Advantage and the Rising Skill Differential." Mimeo, New York, N.Y., Columbia University, 1992 [1992b].

Dixit, Avinash. "Investment and Hysteresis." *Journal of Economic Perspectives*, vol. 6, 1992, pp. 107–32.

The Economist. "Musical Chairs" (Economics Focus column). July 17, 1993, p. 67.

Ethier, Wilfred J. "Higher Dimensional Issues in Trade Theory." In R. Jones and P. Kenen, eds., *Handbook of International Economics*, vol. 1, International Trade. Amsterdam, North-Holland: 1984.

Findlay, Ronald, and Harry Grubert. "Factor Intensities, Technical Progress, and the Terms of Trade." *Oxford Economic Papers*, no. 11, 1959, pp. 111–21.

Freeman, Richard B. "How Much Has De-Unionization Contributed to the Rise in Male Earnings Inequality?" NBER Working Paper Series, no. 3826, Cambridge, Mass., 1991.

Griliches, Zvi. "Capital-Skill Complementarity." *Review of Economics and Statistics*, vol. 51, 1969, pp. 465–68.

Grossman, Gene M. "Imports as a Cause of Injury: The Case of the U.S. Steel Industry." *Journal of International Economics*, vol. 20, 1986, pp. 201–23.

———. "The Employment and Wage Effects of Import Competition in the United States." *Journal of International Economic Integration*, vol. 2, 1987, pp. 1–23.

Harris, John R., and Michael P. Todaro. "Migration, Unemployment, and Development: A Two-Sector Analysis." *American Economic Review*, vol. 60, 1970, pp. 126–42.

Helpman, Elhanan, and Paul R. Krugman. *Market Structure and Foreign Trade*. Cambridge, Mass.: MIT Press, 1985.

Katz, Lawrence F., and Lawrence H. Summers. "Can Interindustry Wage Differentials Justify Strategic Trade Policy?" In R. Feenstra, ed., *Trade Policies for International Competitiveness*. Chicago, Ill.: University of Chicago Press, 1989.

Krueger, Alan B. "How Computers Have Changed the Wage Structure: Evidence and Implications." *Brookings Papers on Economic Activity, Microeconomics*. The Brookings Institution, Washington, D.C., 1993, pp. 209–10.

Lawrence, Robert Z., and Matthew J. Slaughter. "Trade and U.S. Wages: Great Sucking Sound or Small Hiccup?" Faculty Research Working Paper Series, John F. Kennedy School of Government, Harvard University, 1993.

Layard, P. R. G., and A. A. Walters. *Microeconomic Theory*. New York, N.Y.: McGraw-Hill, 1978.

Leamer, Edward E. "Wage Effects of a U.S.-Mexico Free Trade Agreement." National Bureau of Economic Research Working Paper no. 3991. Cambridge, Mass.: NBER, 1992.

Leontief, Wassily W. "Domestic Production and Foreign Trade: The American Capital Position Re-examined." *Proceedings of the American Philosophical Society*, vol. 97, 1953, pp. 332–49.

Levinsohn, James. "Testing the Imports-as-Market-Discipline Hypothesis." *Journal of International Economics*, vol. 35, 1993, pp. 1–22.

Levy, Frank, and Richard J. Murnane. "U.S. Earnings Inequality: A Review of Recent Trends and Proposed Explanations." *Journal of Economic Literature*, vol. 30, 1992, pp. 1333–81.

Lipsey, Robert E. "Foreign Direct Investment in the United States: Changes over Three Decades." NBER Working Paper Series, no. 3581, Cambridge, Mass.: NBER, 1992.

Mincer, Jacob. "Human Capital, Technology, and the Wage Structure: What Do Time Series Show?" NBER Working Paper Series, no. 3581, Cambridge, Mass.: NBER, 1991.

———. "Interindustry Wage Structure." Mimeo, New York, N.Y., Columbia University, 1993.

———. *Studies in Human Capital: Collected Essays of Jacob Mincer*. Hampshire, England: Edward Elgar, 1993.

Mincer, Jacob, and Yoshio Higuchi. "Wage Structures and Labor Turnover in the United States and Japan." *Journal of the Japanese and International Economies*, vol. 2, 1988, pp. 97–133.

Minhas, B. S. "The Homohypallagic Production Function, Factor Intensity Reversals, and the Heckscher-Ohlin Theorem." *Journal of Political Economy*, vol. 70, 1962, pp. 138–56.

Mitchell, Daniel J. B. "Wage Pressures and Labor Shortages: The 1960s and 1980s." *Brookings Papers on Economic Activity*, no. 2. The Brookings Institution, Washington, D.C., 1989, pp. 191–232.

Murphy, Kevin M., and Finis Welch. "The Role of International Trade in Wage Differentials." In M. Kosters, ed., *Workers and Their Wages*. Washington, D.C.: AEI Press, 1991.

Panagariya, Arvind. "Variable Returns to Scale in General Equilibrium Theory Once Again." *Journal of International Economics*, vol. 10, 1980, pp. 499–526.

Passell, Peter. "The Victim Has a Blue Collar, but Free Trade Has an Alibi." *New York Times*, sec. 4, p. 4, August 16, 1992.

Perot, Ross, and Pat Choate. *Save Your Job, Save Our Country: Why NAFTA Must Be Stopped—Now!* New York, N.Y.: Hyperion, 1993.

Revenga, Ana L. "Exporting Jobs: The Impact of Import Competition on Employment and Wages in U.S. Manufacturing." *Quarterly Journal of Economics*, vol. 107, 1992, pp. 255–84.

Rybczynski, T. M. "Factor Endowment and Relative Commodity Prices." *Economica*, vol. 12, 1955, pp. 336–41.

Samuelson, Paul A. "International Trade and the Equalisation of Factor Prices." *Economic Journal* , vol. 58, 1948, pp. 163–84.

———. "International Factor-Price Equalisation Once Again." *Economic Journal*, vol. 59, 1949, pp. 181–97.

———. "A Theory of Induced Innovation Along Kennedy-Weizsacker Lines." *Review of Economics and Statistics*, vol. 47, 1965, pp. 343–56.

———. "A New Revolution at Century's End." Mimeo, Cambridge, Mass., MIT, 1992.

Stolper, Wolfgang, and Paul A. Samuelson. "Protection and Real Wages." *Review of Economic Studies*, vol. 9, 1941, pp. 58–73.

3
Trade and Wages—
What Are the Questions?
Alan V. Deardorff and Dalia S. Hakura

Starting in the early 1970s, real wages in the United States ceased growing at their previous rate and may even have begun to decline. Around 1980, wages of skilled and educated workers began to rise relative to those of unskilled workers, thus leading to growing inequality among working groups.[1] These changes more or less coincided with an increase in the U.S. deficit on international trade, which grew steadily and then rose to unprecedented levels through the first half of the 1980s. Combined with the continued growth of both exports and imports in proportion to output that had occurred throughout the postwar period, these events naturally led to speculation that the cause of the decline in wages, and especially those of unskilled workers relative to skilled, was international trade. In just the past few years, therefore, interest in this age-old topic of the effects of trade on wages has been renewed, and many empirical papers have appeared on the subject in the literatures of both labor economics and international trade. Our purpose here is to have a look at this literature. We will be concerned primarily with how various investigators have framed the question of the effects of trade on wages and whether, once these questions are understood, one would want to know the answers. Our own view is that most of this empirical literature has failed to address the interesting questions and has instead answered easier questions that are of questionable relevance, both to policy and to economic understanding of the world.

We have received helpful comments on earlier drafts from Jagdish Bhagwati, John Bound, George Johnson, Jim Levinsohn, Marvin Kosters, Frank Stafford, Bob Stern, and other participants in both the AEI seminar and a seminar at the University of Michigan.

1. See Kosters, chapter 1 of this volume, for a survey of the literature documenting these changes.

Considerable analytical firepower has been directed at this issue of the empirical relationship between trade and wages. Our concern here will not be to sort out and evaluate the analytical techniques that have been used. Rather, we will try only to clarify what the questions are that these papers have been asking.

We begin in the following section by discussing several theoretical interpretations of the issue of trade and wages—various specific questions that one might expect an empirical investigation to answer. Our purpose is to provide a framework for the later discussion and to indicate that either some of the questions the literature has addressed are not well formed or their answers are not informative. We turn in subsequent sections to a brief survey of some of the major contributions to this literature, organized in terms of these questions.[2]

How Does Trade Affect Wages?

The Question in Theoretical Terms. The question, How does trade affect wages?—or, How has it affected wages over some period of time?—is both a surprising and a natural question to ask from the point of view of an international trade theorist.[3] We trade theorists study the determinants of trade and therefore think of trade as something endogenous, not exogenous. We typically think of trade as arising *because* of differences in wages or labor costs. We are accustomed also, however, to asking how trade affects all sorts of things, including welfare, factor prices, and outputs. Two of our classic theorems from the Heckscher-Ohlin (H-O) model of international trade theory—the factor price equalization (FPE) theorem and the Stolper-Samuelson theorem—deal precisely with the effects of trade on wages and other factor prices.

This suggests that, in any sensible model, the volume of trade

---

2. In chapter 1 of this volume, Kosters has summarized many of the empirical patterns that have been observed in the labor market in recent years, and in chapter 2, Bhagwati and Dehejia have explored alternative theoretical rationales for some of these patterns.

3. It is possible that a labor theorist would have a different take on this than a trade theorist. Trade theorists have a long tradition of general equilibrium analysis and are likely to use that to confront this question. Labor theorists may be more willing to consider labor markets in isolation from the rest of the economy.

and the level of wages are simultaneously determined.[4] To ask about the effects of one upon the other without making clearer the context is not meaningful. Furthermore, as in the trade theorems, one can easily state the relationships in a rigorous and meaningful manner.

Thus, in the FPE theorem, when we say that free trade equalizes factor prices, we are referring to a well-defined situation in which all barriers to trade are eliminated. In that special case of free trade, if a number of other assumptions also hold, including that factors are perfectly mobile across industries and that factor endowments of different countries are sufficiently similar to permit incomplete specialization, then those countries will share the same prices of all factors. It is the *absence of trade barriers,* and not any measure of the volume or terms of trade, that affects factor prices here. This is a testable proposition in principle, although the difficulty of finding situations of truly free trade makes that difficult in practice. Note, however, that the FPE theorem does *not* say that a movement closer to free trade, if that could be defined, would draw factor prices closer together. It is a theorem about a static equilibrium with perfectly free trade; it is not a comparative static proposition.[5]

Similarly, the Stolper-Samuelson theorem refers (depending on the version stated) not to the effects of some ill-defined thing called trade, but rather to the quite specific effects of changing or eliminating trade barriers such as tariffs. Wolfgang Stolper and Paul Samuelson showed that an increase in tariffs, in the context of the two-country, two-good, two-factor H-O model and again under certain assumptions that include factor mobility and incomplete specialization, will raise the real return to the country's scarce factor of production and lower the real return to the abundant factor. Here

---

4. This is assuming, of course, that they can vary at all. If government policy were to constrain trade volumes through quotas or import licensing, then additional adjustments would be required through prices, and if policy were to constrain wages, there would be additional adjustment through employment. But the point is that equilibriums in trade and labor markets, however attained, are simultaneously determined.

5. Deardorff (1986) explored the theoretical difficulty of proving a tendency toward FPE when full FPE does not occur, as when countries move only part way toward free trade. Under the usual assumptions that would be needed for FPE, but without incomplete specialization, it is possible with more than two goods for a move toward free trade to draw factor prices further apart. Thus, while most trade theorists may believe that the FPE theorem is suggestive of a tendency toward FPE when full FPE fails, it is only suggestive. Such a tendency has not been proven theoretically except in very special cases.

again it is not trade per se that alters factor prices, however, but rather the change in protection.

Stolper and Samuelson themselves spoke of the effects of protection on wages, but at the heart of their analysis was a relationship that must hold, under their assumptions, between the prices of goods and the prices of factors. As discussed by Jagdish Bhagwati (1959) and further elaborated by Ronald W. Jones (1965), the essence of the result is an implication of the zero-profit conditions in a two-sector economy. A rise in the relative price of a good must raise the return to the factor used intensively in its production more than in proportion to the price change,[6] and it must lower the return to the other factor. This relationship is today often stated as the Stolper-Samuelson theorem, and often in the form of the change in the prices of goods *causing* the change in the prices of factors. Causation is not really part of the result, however; it is only a relationship that must hold under certain conditions. And even that relationship can fail if those conditions are not met, as for example if there is a change in technology.

In spite of these qualifications, the Stolper-Samuelson theorem has provided the motivation and focus for much of the recent empirical literature dealing with the effects of trade on wages. The empirical observations noted above seem to suggest it, after all. If trade in the United States has grown because trade barriers have been reduced (through successive rounds of trade negotiations under the GATT, for example[7]), then the theorem would seem to predict that the real wage of the scarce factor in the United States, unskilled labor, would fall, while that of our abundant factor, skilled labor, would rise.[8] This may be a natural association, but the theorem does not say that it is *trade* that has these effects; rather it attributes them to the change in

6. This is commonly referred to as the "magnification" effect, after Jones (1965).

7. It is questionable, however, that barriers to trade did in fact fall, especially in the United States in the 1980s. Tariffs did fall slightly as the negotiated reductions of the Tokyo Round were implemented, but a wide variety of nontariff barriers were simultaneously erected and raised. See Deardorff (1991) for a discussion.

8. In fact, even this simple statement is not justified by theory if there are more than two factors. Allowing for capital, land, natural resources, and different types (perhaps more than two) of labor weakens the Stolper-Samuelson theorem considerably, though it still implies at least a weak relationship between factor abundance and the effects of protection on the corresponding factor prices. See Deardorff (1993) for an overview of the theoretical literature on the Stolper-Samuelson theorem.

tariffs or perhaps the change in relative prices. Those studies that have related the changes in factor prices to, say, the volume of trade cannot therefore be said to have been necessarily applying the Stolper-Samuelson theorem.

A final theoretical contribution should be mentioned before we proceed, since many in trade theory would regard it as more relevant than the Stolper-Samuelson theorem for explaining effects on wages in the short run. That is the Specific Factors model, sometimes called the Ricardo-Viner model and reintroduced into the post-Heckscher-Ohlin literature by Samuelson (1971), Jones (1971), Wolfgang Mayer (1974), and Michael Mussa (1974), among others. In that model, at least one factor is immobile among industries, and therefore a different factor price can be paid in each industry. With all factors specific in this way, the price of each factor depends only on the price of the output it helps to produce. If some factors are specific and others not, then the price of the nonspecific factor is the same across industries, but it responds to changes in goods prices differently from the Stolper-Samuelson theorem. In the most common version of the model, for example, capital is specific while labor is mobile within a two-sector economy. A rise in the relative price of one good then raises the real return to capital there, lowers the real return to capital in the other sector, and has an ambiguous effect on the real wage of labor depending on the importance of the more expensive good in the budgets of workers.

These theoretical results, as well as analogous ones that hold with more than two factors, suggest that the determination of wages is not as simple as the Stolper-Samuelson theorem suggests. But note that all of them have wages and other factor prices depending not on trade per se but on prices of goods. These in turn may be determined primarily in world markets, depending on the size of the country, and under special additional assumptions they may even vary systematically with the quantities of trade. But we know of no general and direct relationship between the volume of trade and wages that holds in any general-equilibrium theory of trade.

Finally, we also note that while various models relate wages to prices of goods rather than to trade, they typically relate them to the entire constellation of goods prices, not just to one of them. Only in the most extreme specific-factors model, where all factors of production are immobile across all sectors, are particular wages explainable by only the price of the output they help to produce. This model presumably applies, if at all, only to the very short run. With any mobility of factors across sectors, wages in general equilibrium depend upon all goods prices simultaneously, making any estimation of an empirical relationship problematic.

Taking into account these insights from international trade theory, let us now ask what one can make of the question, "How does trade affect wages?" We suggest that several interpretations, or versions of the question, can be meaningful. We discuss them here, and then look later in the chapter at the extent to which the literature has addressed them.

Consider the question first in the abstract, in theoretical terms and without reference to any particular historical episode. We will discuss how these interpretations and others carry over to empirical work in a moment. Three quite different interpretations can be placed on this question.

How does a reduction in trade barriers affect wages? This interpretation is motivated most directly by the theorems of trade theory. Since trade barriers may plausibly be taken as exogenous, barring political economy considerations, it is a sensible question. The answer may depend on the model used (with or without scale economies, for example); the time horizon (whether labor is mobile across industries, for example); and the pattern and type of trade barriers being considered (unilateral versus multilateral versus minilateral free trade, for example, or reductions in transport costs). But we know the meaning of the question.

How do changes in economic conditions abroad, transmitted to the domestic economy through trade, affect wages? Alternatively, the question could refer to any changes that might take place outside the country to the extent that these changes would, at unchanged trade barriers, lead to an increase in trade. As long as those foreign changes are themselves plausibly independent of events at home, then again this would be a well-defined question. We might for example ask about the effects on domestic wages of a rise in productivity abroad that will be transmitted to the domestic economy through increased trade.

This interpretation works only to the extent that the changes abroad are transmitted to the domestic economy through trade. If trade acts as the only or the primary conduit through which changes in one country affect another, then although the underlying cause of a change in wages is the change in technology abroad, it is also accurate to attribute the changes to trade. For without the increase in trade the domestic response would not have occurred. This is a "but for" interpretation of the effects of trade: "but for the increase in trade caused by the foreign productivity improvement and permitted by unchanged barriers to trade, domestic wages would not have declined."

81

Of course, over the past few decades we have seen the expansion of various other transmission mechanisms through which countries are dependent on one another. Thus it is no longer true, if it ever was, that all international effects are channeled through trade. International flows of capital, both financial and real, are increasingly important, as are flows of other sorts of trade such as services, and to a lesser extent migration of labor. It cannot be assumed that if trade were somehow prevented from expanding, then a country would be insulated from all changes abroad.

How do wages respond differently to changes in economic conditions at home when international trade is allowed to change too, as compared with being held constant? The but-for form of the second question suggests a third. Consider an exogenous change that originates *within* the home country and that raises imports. It could for example be an increase in total demand for goods, regardless of source, part of which shows up as an increase in imports. One can ask what would have happened instead if imports had not been permitted to increase. If wages would have gone up more, or down less, with imports somehow held constant, then one might attribute this wage effect to trade. Presumably this argument could be sensitive to the method that is implicitly used to hold imports constant, including how exports would be treated. But given that method, this is a well-defined interpretation of what trade means for wages.

To continue the above example, an increase in total demand will normally raise imports at the same time that it raises demands for other goods and factors. One could, however, place quantitative restrictions on all imports, so that their quantities would not rise but their prices would. One could alternatively vary tariffs on every import to achieve the same result. This would be a substantial difference in policy regime, and the implications for domestic wages would likely be very different. The third question seeks to identify this difference. These are the wage effects of the increase in total demand that would have occurred but for the permitted increase in trade.

As we will see, the literature on trade and wages does not usually answer exactly any of these three questions. Instead, various authors have answered questions that are related to these, but are not the same. The first is another "but for" question that in effect combines the second and third questions above and includes both of them as special cases:

Regarding any exogenous change, at home or abroad, that might affect trade or wages, how would wages respond differently if the volume of trade were held constant? This is the most general interpretation possible: But for any change in trade, how would wages have behaved differently? It does not concern itself with the underlying causes of the changes in both trade and wages, including whether they are foreign or domestic. As such it is likely to be the easiest to answer empirically, since these causes do not have to be identified. But although it is a well-defined question, its broad scope makes it less interesting than any of the others. Its answer will be different for different situations, depending on the underlying causes for the change in trade. Unless one is seriously considering clamping down on the volume of trade, knowing how such a drastic policy would alter the course of wages does not have a great deal of policy relevance.

All the preceding questions, excepting the first, have used the volume of trade as the benchmark for identifying the effects of trade. Yet only in a small, open economy is it theoretically correct to take conditions of international trade as given, and therefore as a possible exogenous cause of changes in wages. In a small, open economy it is not trade volumes, but rather international prices, that are independent of domestic behavior. In such an economy, the volume of trade is entirely dependent on how domestic firms and consumers respond to international prices and to other domestic variables. It therefore seems inappropriate to define the effects of trade on wages in that model in terms of any measure of trade volume. Recognizing this, several investigators have used international prices, instead of trade volumes, as their explanatory variables. This suggests yet another variation on the "but for" question:

Regarding any exogenous change that might affect trade or wages, how would wages respond differently if the international prices were held constant? For a truly small, open economy, this question is an improvement over the preceding one, since it will attribute to trade only those changes that can alter world prices. Changes originating only domestically will be viewed as having zero effects. The effects of changes that originate both at home and abroad, however—such as a worldwide change in technology—will still be attributed to trade, much as in the other "but for" interpretations above. And here the question is perhaps even less plausible than in the others: But for the changes in world prices, how would wages have behaved differently? For it seems to assume that trade policy could in fact be used to hold prices constant, and that may not be true.[9]

---

9. Actually, it may only be the domestic equivalents of international prices that must be held constant. If so this can in principle be achieved by suitable variation in taxes and subsidies on exports and imports.

Empirical Implementation. In dealing with various empirical episodes, each of the first three interpretations above could in principle be addressed. One could ask: (a) what the wage effects of a particular trade liberalization would be, or would have been; (b) what the wage effects in one country are for a particular change such as a productivity improvement in another country, these effects presumably being transmitted through trade; and (c) what portion of a wage decline due, say, to lagging productivity at home could have been prevented had the volume of trade been held fixed. There have been many studies of the first type, but most have addressed the question from a different perspective than that of the trade and wages literature considered here. Most of these studies have used computable general equilibrium (CGE) models, applying them to things like the Tokyo Round and the NAFTA, and they have typically examined these effects ex ante rather than ex post. We will not consider them further here.[10] The only studies we know that have explicitly tried to examine the effects of trade liberalization ex post are by Bhagwati (1991a,b) and by Robert Lawrence and Matthew Slaughter (1993). The second and third questions do not appear to have been asked in the literature at all, perhaps because of the difficulty of isolating—or even settling upon—a single source of exogenous change.

Instead most of the empirical studies have asked one of the more general but-for questions, controlling for the effect of either a quantity or a price of trade, and not specifying the ultimate source of change in either. Some studies ask: (d) How have wages responded to the increased trade volumes of a particular period? In other words, if the volume of trade had been held fixed over the same period, how would wages have been different? Others ask: (e) How have wages responded to the changes in world prices over some period? This is to ask the same thing, but for prices instead of trade volumes.

As indicated, some empirical studies focus on episodes of changes in trade volume, others on changes in prices. A number of studies, however, put their focus more on particular changes in wages and try to explain them. To the extent that they try to explain the wage changes in relation to trade, this different focus has the same alternative interpretations available as before. That is, for example, if there has been a change in tariffs at the same time as the wage change being examined, then one can ask whether the former caused the latter. Or, using a but-for interpretation, one can ask whether

---

10. See Srinivasan and Whalley (1986) for a survey of a broad spectrum of CGE models, and Brown (1992) for a more recent survey of models applied to the NAFTA.

holding trade quantities or prices constant would have prevented the wage change that was observed. This latter interpretation is a little awkward, since it requires an arbitrary baseline for comparison.

Looking only at trade to answer such a question is suspect, however. Many possible reasons can cause wages to change. If one had looked at all of them along with trade, using a comparable methodology for each, then one might well have explained either more or less of the wage change than actually occurred. One would then have to conclude that something was wrong, and perhaps to scale downward or upward all the separate estimates. By looking at trade only, one does not have the chance to find out what the errors are. Therefore it is surely better to explain the wage change by looking as far as possible at all the contributing factors at once.

A number of studies have taken this approach, estimating a wage equation that includes a variety of explanatory variables. These, including trade, are then evaluated in terms of their respective contributions to this regression. This approach contains a number of problems, however, including that the wage equations themselves are not usually well motivated by theory.

First, unless one focuses on trade policies rather than on trade per se, the trade variable is bound to be an endogenous one that is simultaneously determined with wages.[11] Techniques for dealing with this simultaneity exist, of course, but they require more information about the structure of the economy than most investigators have.

Second, once multiple explanatory variables are included, the "but for" interpretation that we discussed above becomes less clear. Are we asking how wages would have behaved differently if only trade were held fixed, or are we also controlling for the other right-hand-side variables? The usual procedure is to speak of trade's contribution to the explanation of wages, but since trade is endogenous, it is not clear what this means. Does it mean that if trade had been held fixed, then the wage would have changed by a certain percentage less? That would be a reasonable statement, but is it really warranted by the estimation? When endogenous volumes or prices of trade enter as explanatory variables along with other exogenous variables that could themselves affect those volumes and prices, then the separate roles of both must be intertwined and difficult to interpret without estimating a structural model.

Examples. To illustrate some of these points more concretely, it is

---

11. Even trade policies, such as tariffs and quotas, may be endogenous for political economy reasons, of course. This is especially important to take into account in estimation across industries.

helpful to consider several theoretical examples of exogenous changes that would affect both trade and wages. These examples are chosen because they all lead to roughly the changes in trade and wages that have been observed, even though the exogenous changes that initiate them are quite different. They therefore underscore the point that looking at trade and wages alone cannot be enough to identify what is going on.[12]

There are five examples, all in the context of an H-O model of trade, with two factors, skilled S and unskilled U labor, producing a skill-intensive, high-tech good H and an unskill-intensive–low-tech good L. There is also an even more skill-intensive nontraded good N in the last of the five examples. Prices of goods and factors are p and w with obvious subscripts. The country, in each case, is small.

Example 1: tariff cut on imports of L. Consider the removal of a tariff on imports of the unskill-intensive–low-tech good. Effects on factor markets are shown in figure 3–1. The solid lines indicate unit-value isoquants and resulting employment and wages of factors in the presence of the tariff. The broken lines show the situation after the tariff is removed. The country's endowment is fixed at point E. Tariff removal shifts the L-isoquant outward, causing the wages needed for diversification to rise for S and fall for U. Effects on production and trade are shown in figure 3–2, panel A, which is the familiar textbook depiction of a tariff in terms of production possibilities and community indifference curves. Clearly, the tariff cut has raised skilled wages relative to unskilled wages and expanded the volume of trade.

Example 2: foreign expansion in production of L. Suppose that production of the low-tech good expands abroad, either because of factor accumulation there or because of technical change that occurs abroad but not at home. This will cause the relative price of the low-tech good to fall on world markets. Using good H as numeraire, effects on factor markets are exactly the same as in figure 3–1, the L-isoquant shifting outward. Effects on outputs and trade are shown in figure 3–2, panel B. Again, the foreign expansion has raised the skill differential and increased the volume of trade.

Example 3: technical progress at home in production of H. Let there now be a Hicks-neutral improvement in the technology for producing the high-tech good H in the home country only. This will shift the

---

12. These are not by any means the only examples possible. Bhagwati and Dehejia (1993), for example, provide an explanation in terms of increasing labor turnover among the unskilled.

FIGURE 3–1
FACTOR-MARKET EFFECTS OF A TARIFF CUT

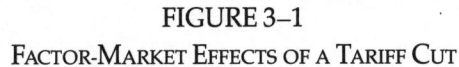

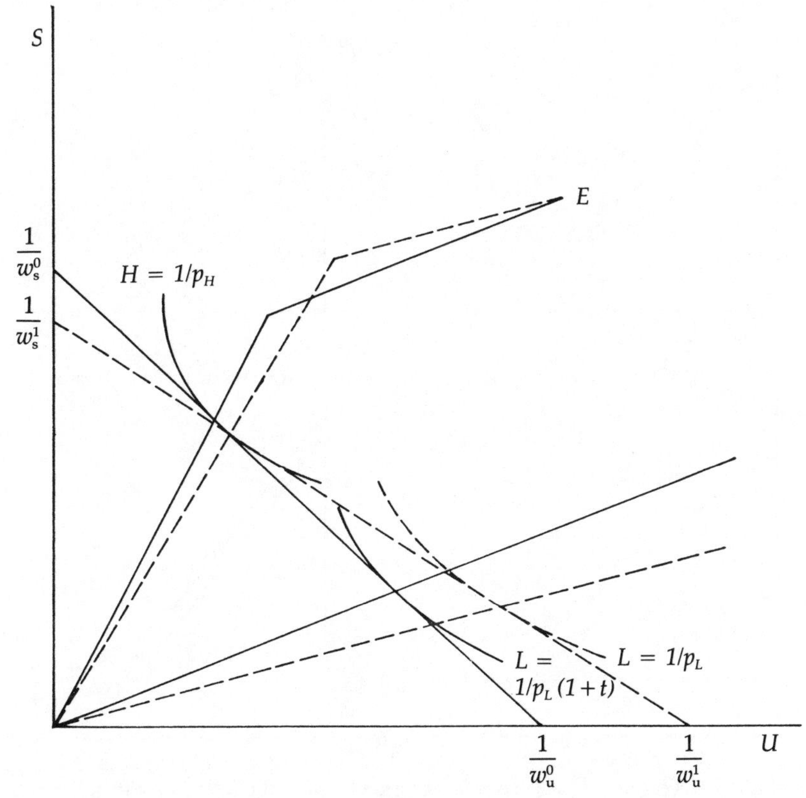

S

$\dfrac{1}{w_s^0}$

$\dfrac{1}{w_s^1}$

$H = 1/p_H$

E

$L = 1/p_L$

$L = \dfrac{1}{p_L\,(1+t)}$

$\dfrac{1}{w_u^0}$ $\dfrac{1}{w_u^1}$ U

NOTE: Solid lines show unit-value isoquants, unit isocost line, and allocation of factor endowment E for skilled (S) and unskilled (U) labor in the presence of a tariff on the low-tech good L. Broken lines show the same in the absence of the tariff. This indicates that the tariff cut causes the skilled wage to rise, the unskilled wage to fall, and resources to shift into the high-tech sector H.
SOURCE: Authors.

H-isoquant inward, toward the origin, rather than the L-isoquant outward, but the effects on factor markets are otherwise so similar to the previous cases that we do not show them separately. Effects on output and trade are shown in figure 3–2, panel C. This particular case of technical progress therefore has also raised the skill differential and increased the volume of trade.

87

FIGURE 3-2
Examples of Output and Trade Effects

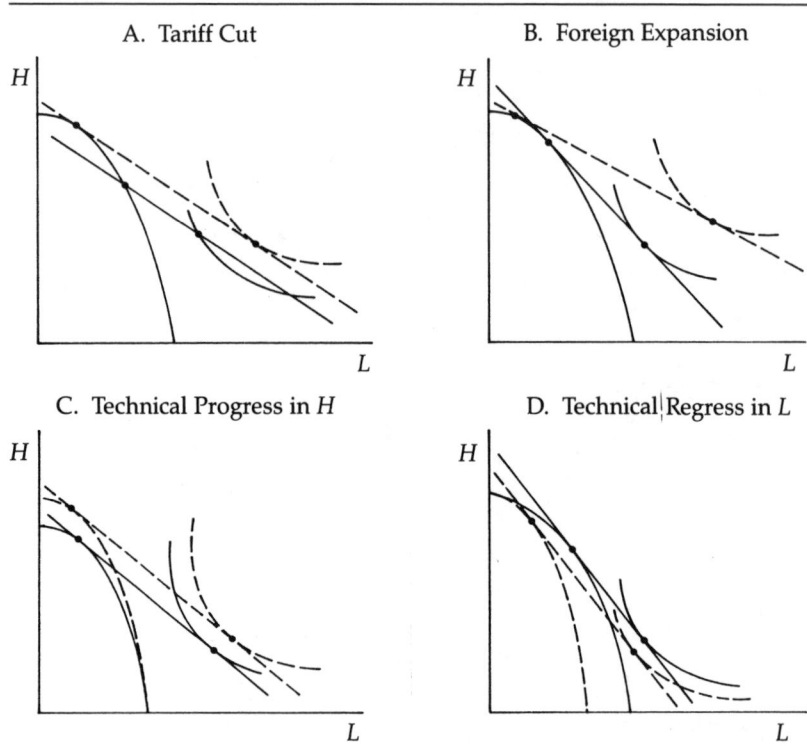

A. Tariff Cut

B. Foreign Expansion

C. Technical Progress in *H*

D. Technical Regress in *L*

Note: Panels show production possibility frontiers for a high-tech good *H* and a low-tech good *L*, together with price lines and community indifference curves that indicate production and consumption. Solid lines denote the initial situation, broken lines the situation after the indicated change. In all four cases, for very different reasons, production of *H* expands and *L* contracts while imports of *L* increase.
Source: Authors.

Example 4: technical regress at home in production of L. If instead there were a deterioration in some technology, one could still get essentially the same effects.[13] Suppose there is a Hicks-neutral worsening in the technology for producing the low-tech good *L*, again in the home country only. This will shift the *L*-isoquant outward, exactly as in figure 3-1. Effects on output and trade are shown in figure 3-2,

---

13. An institutional change or a regulation that lowers productivity could also have this effect.

FIGURE 3-3

FACTOR-MARKET EFFECTS OF A RISE IN EXPENDITURE

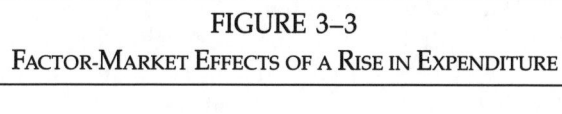

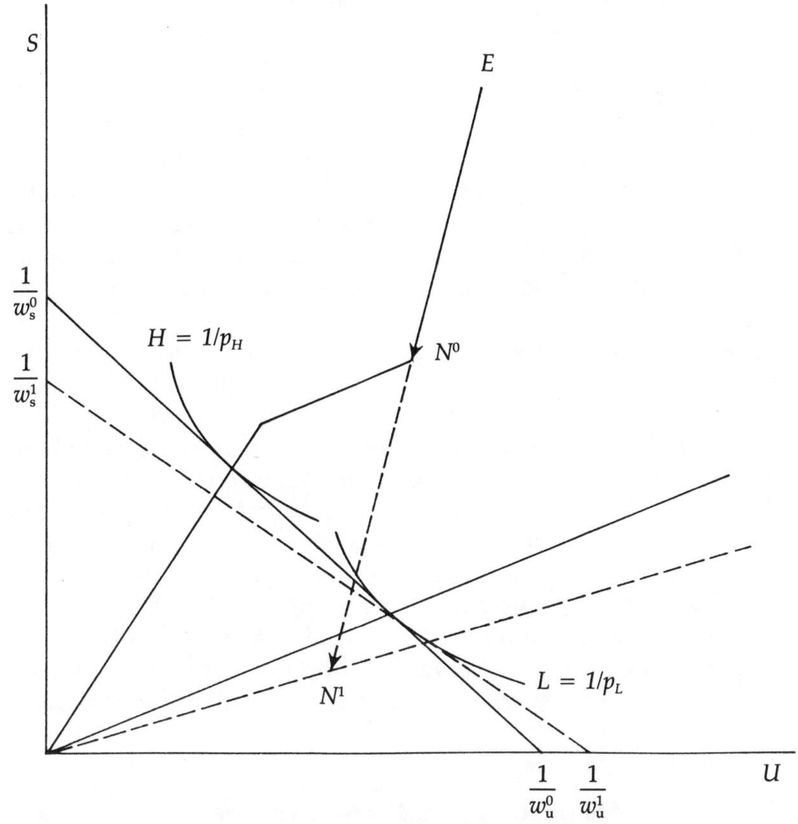

NOTE: Solid lines show initial positions of unit-value isoquants for two traded goods, L and H; a unit isocost line; and an allocation of factor endowment E to those two industries plus a nontraded industry N. Broken lines show the effects of an increase in expenditure that requires greater production of the nontraded good, leading to complete specialization in traded good L, a rise in the skilled wage, and a fall in the unskilled wage.
SOURCE: Authors.

panel D. Once again, the skill differential widens and the volume of trade increases.

Example 5: rise in expenditure at home. In figure 3–3 we add a nontraded good, production of which, in the initial equilibrium, uses up an amount of the factors indicated by the solid arrow pointing

89

inward from the endowment point E. N^0 therefore indicates the amounts of factors that remain for production of the two traded goods, leading to factor prices and employment much as before. Now suppose that total expenditure on all goods rises, earned income remaining constant. At the macroeconomic level, this will of course create a trade deficit. At the microeconomic level, increased expenditure will raise demand for the nontraded good, production of which will therefore now require larger amounts of both factors. The arrow extending from E is therefore lengthened, leaving only the factors at N^1 available for producing traded goods. In the example shown, this so reduces the availability of skilled labor that the economy moves to complete specialization in L, and factor prices change. Once again, the skilled wage rises, both in real terms and relative to the unskilled wage.

The message of these five examples is simply this: there are many possible reasons for the skill differential to increase at the same time that the volume of trade increases. Showing that the two are related empirically does not therefore mean that trade is somehow responsible for the change in wages. If the examples were carried further, it would undoubtedly also be true that the wage changes would have been different had trade been held constant by some form of trade intervention. Nevertheless, the causes of the changes, except in example 1, would have been something other than trade.

With these uncertainties about both the accuracy and the interpretation of attempts to estimate the effects of trade on wages, let us now turn to our survey of the major contributions that have been made.

Studies of Effects of Trade Volumes

Several studies in the past few years have attempted to infer wage changes from changes in trade volumes. We look at two groups of them. The first group infers wage changes indirectly by first calculating the labor content of changes in trade. That is, they use the factor requirements of production to infer the effects of trade on the quantity of labor demanded. Thus the primary emphasis of these studies is on a quantity-quantity relationship. Effects on wages are then deduced in a second step, by combining the quantity estimates with elasticities, usually from other sources. In contrast, the second group of studies that uses trade volumes looks at wages more directly, typically estimating a wage equation that includes trade volumes among other explanatory variables.

Calculations of the Labor Content of Changes in Demand. George Borjas, Richard Freeman, and Lawrence Katz (1991) do the most straightforward study of this type. For various periods in which the quantities of trade changed, they regard the labor needed to produce exports as being subtracted from the available domestic labor supply. The labor needed to produce substitutes for imports is viewed as additions to the labor supply. Using disaggregated data on trade and on the employment of various occupations in different industries, they therefore attribute the changes in this labor supply to trade during the 1980s. This terminology, identifying as changes in supply what were really changes in demand for labor, is apparently motivated by the desire in the second part of the analysis to link the quantity changes to wages on the basis of known responses to supply shifts. We will use net supply and net demand interchangeably in our discussion of this particular study.

We know of course that the U.S. trade deficit expanded dramatically during the first half of the 1980s. Therefore the Borjas, Freeman, and Katz methodology is guaranteed to generate the result for that period that the total demand for labor would decrease. Since the study does not allow for any other changes in the aggregate demand for labor that might have occurred during the same period, its implications for effects on total employment and wages should therefore be discounted.

The focus of Borjas, Freeman, and Katz, however, is not so much on the total labor market as on the different groups of labor within it. Here their calculations identify unskilled labor as being the group with the greatest increase in supply due to trade. From that they conclude that trade must have lowered the relative employment of unskilled labor—a conclusion that strikes us as valid, though only within the context of the but-for interpretation discussed above. That is, without attempting to identify the reasons for the changes in trade that took place during the 1980s, Borjas, Freeman, and Katz correctly identify the relative changes in demand for different types of labor that could be attributed to that trade. But for these changes in trade—if the changes in trade had been prevented by, say, changes in trade barriers—the demand for unskilled labor would have been substantially greater than it was.

The last link in the analysis, from changes in labor supply and demand to changes in wages, is perhaps more tenuous. Their approach is simply to multiply the notional changes in labor supply by selected elasticities taken from regressions they and others have estimated. Thus, in effect, they treat the labor market as though it could be solved in partial equilibrium. This is inconsistent with much that we know from trade theory of how general-equilibrium models behave. In the H-O model, for example, under the assumptions that lead to the FPE and Stolper-Samuelson theorems, factor prices depend directly on output prices through the zero-profit conditions, and they do *not* depend on factor supplies independently of goods prices.[14] With less intersectoral mobility of factors, as in the specific factors model, factor prices do depend on factor supplies as well as on goods prices, but the nature of that dependence depends crucially on the pattern of factor mobility. Only in the most extreme specific factors model, where *all* factors are immobile, can factor prices be inferred in a simple way from factor supplies. Therefore we would not place too much credence in the Borjas, Freeman, and Katz estimates of effects on relative wages.

Their analysis of changes in factor demands, however, is nonetheless useful for indicating in broad terms the directions of change in factor prices that are associated with trade. What they do in their calculations of the effects on net labor demand is to construct the factor-content of the change in trade between two general equilibriums. A theoretical model by Alan Deardorff and Robert Staiger (1988) showed this to be correlated with the changes in factor prices that underlie those equilibriums if technology and preferences are held constant.[15] Thus by showing that the changes in trade in the 1980s involved a decrease in the relative demand for unskilled labor, Borjas, Freeman, and Katz also provide incidental evidence that the same changes in trade were associated with a fall in the relative wage of unskilled labor, relative to what would have occurred without the changes in trade.

What this means exactly depends on what caused trade to change, and Borjas, Freeman, and Katz do not identify that. To take just two possibilities, consider the theoretical examples 2 and 3

---

14. This, in fact, is the central message of the FPE theorem.

15. Deardorff and Staiger (1988) use a simple, multi-sector, perfectly competitive, general equilibrium model to derive several relationships that must hold between changes in factor prices and changes in the factor content of trade between two trading equilibriums with constant technology and preferences. The most general result is a positive correlation between relative changes in the factor content of trade, appropriately normalized, and proportional changes in factor prices. Thus, while it is not true that, say, an increase in the unskilled-labor content of net exports must necessarily be associated with an increase in the wage of unskilled labor in general equilibrium, it must nonetheless be true that, if factor prices change at all, then there is an average positive relationship between the factor contents of *all* factors and the changes in their factor prices.

discussed above. In example 2, the increase in trade was due to an expansion of output of the low-tech good abroad. Since technology and preferences at home are constant in this example, the factor content calculation is indicative of the changes in factor prices that are also caused by this change, and which could have been prevented by fixing the quantities of trade and thus insulating the domestic market. In example 3, on the other hand, the cause is a change in technology at home. In this case the change in factor content indicates not the wage effects of that change itself, but rather the difference in effects of the technical change on wages if trade either is or is not allowed to change as well.

Note that in both of these cases the insight from the H-O model that goods prices and factor prices must go together continues to be valid. In example 2 the effect on wages occurs only to the extent that the foreign expansion alters world prices. In example 3, however, the relevant price change is not the observable one caused by the change in technology, but rather the presumably unobservable difference in prices that *would have* occurred without a change in trade.

A second important study of this sort is that of Kevin Murphy and Finis Welch (1991). Like Borjas, Freeman, and Katz, they calculate the effects of changes in sectoral trade balances on the demand for labor at fixed prices,[16] and they use that to infer the employment changes that can be attributed to changes in trade. They do not connect these employment changes directly with wages, although they do argue that the patterns they calculate for employment changes match the patterns of wage changes.

The biggest difference between Murphy and Welch on the one hand and Borjas, Freeman, and Katz on the other is the treatment of aggregate demand. As noted above, Borjas, Freeman, and Katz assume that any increase in imports reduces demand for domestic labor. In a period of rising trade deficit such as the early 1980s, this ensures that they will calculate a drop in employment. In contrast, Murphy and Welch recognize that an increased trade deficit is likely to reflect an increase in demand, and they therefore assume that an increase in the trade deficit has an additional, expansionary effect on aggregate demand. Thus an increase in net imports in a particular

---

16. They refer to their calculations more appropriately as reflecting changes in demand, rather than supply, of labor. Regarding supply, they also provide an important argument that supply changes cannot account for the changes in wages that have been observed. They look for and fail to find the negative correlation between wage and employment changes that would be needed for changes in supply to drive wages.

sector reduces labor demand in that sector, but at the same time it increases demand for goods and therefore labor across the economy. With this assumption, Murphy and Welch get a mixture of expansions and contractions in different sectors, rather than the more or less uniform contraction of demand that must characterize the Borjas, Freeman, and Katz calculations for the early 1980s.

This change in assumptions implies also a change in the nature of the question that the two studies implicitly address. Borjas, Freeman, and Katz implicitly compare employment to what it would have been if trade had been held fixed by policy and if aggregate spending nonetheless expanded by the amount that it in fact did. With trade deficits prevented and the increase in aggregate spending bottled up inside the U.S. economy, one gets a much greater expansion of employment than in fact occurred, and one attributes the shortfall from that expansion to trade. Murphy and Welch, however, compare employment to what it would have been if trade were fixed *and* if aggregate spending were prevented from increasing. The shortfall from this less expansionary path is of course much smaller.

Which of these approaches is more appropriate depends on how trade and aggregate spending are related. If one believes, for example, that trade flows could have been frozen by trade policy, including preventing the increase in the trade deficit of the early 1980s, without interfering with the growth of aggregate real spending, then the Borjas, Freeman, and Katz calculation is correct. If, conversely, one views the expanding trade deficit as the reason why aggregate demand could expand at all in what quickly became a fully employed economy, then the Murphy-Welch calculation is correct. We incline to the latter view.

Once again, however, it is important to understand what question was being addressed. Murphy and Welch attribute to trade both the sectoral expansions and contractions that corresponded to changed exports and imports, and the total expansion of aggregate demand that might not have been possible without trade. There is no sense, however, that either the sectoral changes or the aggregate change themselves were the result of changes in trade policy or of changes that originated abroad and were transmitted to the home market through trade. Quite the contrary, once the change in aggregate spending is recognized by Murphy and Welch, it seems most likely that both sets of changes arose in large part from the changed macroeconomic policies of the early Reagan administration. The calculation of trade effects indicates only how the Reagan policies may have affected U.S. labor markets differently in the presence of trade compared with what would have been possible in its absence.

94

Several other studies have used variants of the approaches of Borjas, Freeman, and Katz (1991) and Murphy and Welch (1991). Katz and Murphy (1992) apply a modified version of the Borjas, Freeman, Katz methodology directly to the United States from 1963 to 1987, and they focus especially on effects on different demographic groups based on sex and levels of education. John Bound and George Johnson (1991, 1992) also take off from the work of these authors, though in a variation that does not look so directly at international trade.

Seeking to evaluate alternative explanations for the observed changes in relative wages, Bound and Johnson group the trade effects of these other authors together with other possible shifts in demand. Rather than looking at the factor content of trade or of other demand shifts, however, they measure the actual shifts in industry employment, then use initial shares of different labor groups to calculate the implied changes in demands for different types of labor. Although this calculation, like those of the previous authors, accords well with observed changes in relative wages, Bound and Johnson argue that it inappropriately holds constant the shares of the different labor groups in the labor force. When they instead make a correction for these changes, then their calculation fails to generate changes in net labor demand that match with observations of the relative wages.

Bound and Johnson therefore conclude that changes in demand, including changes in trade, cannot explain the puzzle. In another part of their analysis, therefore, they examine changes in technology, and they conclude by attributing the larger part of the changes in relative wages to changes in technology that have increased the need for skilled labor.

Other Studies Relating Wages to Trade Volumes. A number of studies have estimated the relationship between trade volumes and wages more directly. Typically, these studies have estimated one or more wage equations with measures of trade volumes or trade balances among the explanatory variables on the right-hand side. Our main criticism of this approach has already been indicated. General-equilibrium theory does not imply such a relationship except in the very short run, and instead suggests that wages are determined by prices. Nonetheless, it is again possible to provide a loose theoretical justification for this approach in terms of the theoretical correlation between the factor content of trade and wages shown by Alan Deardorff and Robert Staiger (1988). In this sense, however, it would be preferable to use the factor content of changes in trade, and not trade itself, as the explanatory variable.

95

A first such study is Katz and Ana Revenga (1989). They look at U.S. and Japanese relative wages and regress them on the aggregate trade imbalance and other explanatory variables. The question here is the same we have discussed before: whether wages would have been different but for certain changes in trade. In this sense, they identify trade as one of several causes of the changes in relative wages that were observed. In particular, they find that a high U.S. trade deficit helps the relative wages of educated and experienced workers in the United States, while favoring new entrants to the labor market in Japan.

Freeman and Katz (1991) examine U.S. wages in unionized versus nonunionized sectors. While they do not calculate the factor content of trade in the manner of some of the previous studies, they do allow trade to play a role. They relate changes in wages to changes in sales, and they decompose sales into three components that focus respectively on domestic sales, exports, and imports. They find that the industry wage structure does respond to changes in sales, with comparable contributions from each of these three components. Thus trade matters for wages in the same way as domestic sales. Regarding unionization, they find a greater sensitivity of wages to sales in unionized than in nonunionized sectors.

Another study by Murphy and Welch (1992) provides a much broader explanation of wages in relation to trade and other explanatory variables. They devote a great deal of attention to careful and elaborate econometric technique in ways that we will not attempt to cover here. The end result is that they find certain trade variables to be significant determinants of wages, though certainly not the only determinants or necessarily the most important. Murphy and Welch are quite explicit that, while they believe that they have established the importance for wages of shifts in demand, they have not been able to identify the primary cause of those shifts. It could be trade, but it could also as easily be skill-biased technical progress.

From our point of view, while these conclusions and the arguments leading to them are impressive, we find it difficult to know how the conclusions regarding trade and technical progress fit together. It seems plausible, for example, that technical progress could have altered wages, both total and relative, among different skill groups. But that same progress would surely also have altered trade. When trade is identified as a separate explanatory variable, what does this mean? That the effects of technical progress are being considered under the assumption that trade does not change? That trade is being considered under the assumption that technology does not change? If both of these, then what about the effects of technology when trade *is* allowed to change? We admit to being confused here to a degree that did not arise with the simpler studies.

We close this section with mention of a final study that also relates wages directly to trade, but in quite a different way. Steven Davis (1992) looks across a large number of countries to see whether relative wage structures in those countries have converged or diverged over time. He finds that they diverged. After controlling for year-specific effects, however, and allowing for the role of trade as a fraction of GDP, he finds that the more open countries, in terms of this trade share, have converging relative wages.

We mention this study last because it is one of the clearest in terms of the question it asks: Does greater openness to international trade cause a country's factor prices to converge to those of its trading partners? As we have noted, a positive answer to this question is not in fact implied by the FPE theorem, even though it may be suggestive of this result. Further, we could quibble with the use of the trade share of GDP as a measure of openness.[17] Still, it is refreshing to find a question so clearly asked and answered.

Studies of Effects of Prices

We have said that general equilibrium trade theory explains wages in terms of prices, not volumes of trade. Several studies have recognized this fact and have used it as the basis for explaining wages. Unfortunately, it does not follow from the existence of a theoretically sound relationship between prices and wages that estimating it is useful. Unless we know the sources of the price change, or unless the prices themselves are likely to be exogenous to the other behaviors we wish to study, knowing how they are related to wages may not be useful.

Consider two examples from other contexts, in one of which a price change is plausibly exogenous, and in the other of which it is not. First, suppose that the price change we were considering was the increase in the price of oil in 1973. Suppose further that this price change was the result of a deliberate action by a group of countries and is not best understood as a response to other changes in the world economy. Therefore it may make good sense to use economic analysis to determine the effects that this price increase may have had, including on the level and structure of wages. It is reasonable to ask how wages would have behaved differently had the oil price not risen.

---

17. A geographically large country like the United States, for example, would have a lower trade to GDP ratio than a smaller country just because of its size, even if its trade barriers were nonexistent.

In contrast, however, consider the more general nominal price increases of the 1970s, which were driven not by decisions about prices but by the overheated economies of the Western world. Recalling the largely fruitless debates about "demand pull" versus "cost push" inflation, it would surely be inappropriate to view these price increases as in any sense coming from outside the system or as being causes of changes in wages. Surely an interactive system was operating, in which prices and wages were both responding to other forces, and the forces too were inside the system. A regression of wages on prices might have worked well in that situation, but it would not have told us anything useful about the policies that might have been used to slow that movement. It would not have told us, in particular, how wages would have changed in the absence of the price changes, since the latter could not have been removed without also removing the more primary causes that were acting on both. A better approach would have been to identify these primary causes and study their effects on both prices and wages simultaneously.

With those caveats, let us look at the studies that have used international prices to explain domestic wages.

The first study we will consider is by Gene Grossman (1987). This is actually an expansion of a 1986 study by Grossman that considers only the steel industry. Grossman estimates reduced form equations for both employment and wages in a number of industries, with import prices included among the explanatory variables. He finds strong evidence of import prices mattering for employment in only one out of eight industries, and for wages in only two out of eight industries.

Revenga (1992) performs a similar analysis, using improved data on import prices and employing an instrumental variables estimation strategy. She is able to find statistically significant effects of import prices on both employment and wages, but for all industries together, not separately, since she pools them under the surprising assumption that all industries would share the same coefficients. She too finds the effects on wages to be much smaller in magnitude than the effects on employment.

The reason for these results, as their authors are well aware, could be that labor is more mobile among sectors of the economy than their models allowed for. In order to obtain manageable estimating equations, both Grossman and Revenga assume that there are separate supply curves for labor to each sector, a minor variation on the specific factors model. This is not implausible, perhaps, but it is contrary to the assumptions of the H-O model of trade. Most of us would regard the assumptions of the H-O model as too extreme in this regard, but the results of Grossman and Revenga suggest that the general-equilibrium, mobile-labor H-O model may have more to recommend it than we thought.

Only a few studies have taken the H-O model seriously as the basis for empirical analysis. Bhagwati (1991a,b) does this, arguing that what matters for factor prices are goods prices, à la the Stolper-Samuelson theorem, and producing empirical evidence that the U.S. terms of trade seem to have behaved in a manner opposite to what is required. A later study by Lawrence and Slaughter (1993) also analyzes this question in much greater depth. They provide a variety of empirical arguments why the changes in goods prices that have been observed cannot account for the observed changes in factor prices. These include: (1) the observation that real wages did not in fact fall in terms of producer prices—as they would have done if the Stolper-Samuelson mechanism had been driving them—but only in terms of consumer prices; (2) several arguments as to what caused consumer prices to differ as they did from producer prices, and why this was not due to trade; and (3) several additional observations that are inconsistent with a Stolper-Samuelson shift in favor of skilled-labor–intensive goods. One such observation is that the ratio of skilled to unskilled workers in manufacturing increased during the 1980s, instead of decreasing, as would have been expected from such a Stolper-Samuelson shift.[18] Second, they note, as did Bhagwati (1991), that relative prices of skill-intensive goods did not rise during that period, but seem rather to have fallen slightly. They argue therefore that observed changes in wages have been consistent with technological improvements that have favored skilled-labor–intensive sectors, and indeed that have been biased in favor of skilled-labor employment.[19]

We find these arguments ingenious and compelling. They rest so heavily on the general-equilibrium model of trade theory that they do not lend themselves to the sorts of econometric analysis that have been used in most of the other studies we have looked at. For that reason they may be slow to gain acceptance among the contributors to that literature. And even for trade economists, this much reliance on the strong implications of the two-sector, H-O model leaves us somewhat uncomfortable. Nonetheless, we admire the efforts made by these authors to examine the data so carefully in accordance with what that economic theory implies.

---

18. See figure 3–1.

19. Example 3 above illustrates such a technical change favoring skill-intensive goods, but does not include this bias. The bias is needed in order to account for the observation that ratios of skilled to unskilled labor increased.

Notice again the question Lawrence and Slaughter have addressed. Has the behavior of wages and prices been consistent with the implications, and thus the assumptions, of the Stolper-Samuelson theorem? Their answer is no, thus implying that one or more of those assumptions is invalid. Their choice for that assumption is the constancy of technology, and they pose an additional question that they answer in the affirmative: has the behavior of wages and prices been consistent with technical progress favoring skilled labor? These questions may not appear to be directed precisely at the issue of how trade has affected wages, but in fact the study seems to have come closer to resolving that issue than most other approaches.

Studies of Protection and Wages

The most straightforward question we asked at the start was how changes in protection would affect wages. As we have seen, most of the literature on trade and wages has not asked this question. Two recent studies, however, do ask it.

The first is by Noel Gaston and Daniel Trefler (1992). Looking across industries, they regress wages on levels of protection, both tariffs and nontariff barriers (NTBs), and ask whether wages are higher or lower in more protected sectors. The key to their technique is that they control for worker characteristics, so that their results provide comparisons of identical workers. They find that wages are negatively correlated with levels of tariffs, but positively correlated with NTBs. That is, wages are highest where tariffs are lowest but where NTBs are highest.[20] Unfortunately, since these are cross-industry regressions, they do not tell us how protection would cause wages to change.

The other study is that of Edward Leamer (1992). We mention it in this section because it deals ostensibly with what effects the NAFTA would have on wages. Thus the question again is clear—how will the removal of tariffs between the United States and Mexico (Leamer did not consider Canada) change wages in the two countries?

Leamer's approach to this question is characteristically original, but it actually has little to do with this question. In a long paper with a number of other useful elements as well, he argues that the NAFTA

---

20. The latter finding, that NTBs are highest in sectors where wages are highest, accords well with the observation by Deardorff and Haveman (1993) that administered protection, such as antidumping duties and countervailing duties, are used in sectors with higher than average wages.

will open up the U.S. market to labor-intensive competition, and that the effects of this competition can be understood by analogy with the increased competition that has already occurred in recent decades. Like Lawrence and Slaughter, he insists that wage effects can only be inferred from price changes. He then sets out first to predict the price changes that a NAFTA would entail, then to transform the price changes into wage changes by estimating Stolper-Samuelson effects.

To predict price changes, he first regresses actual price changes over recent decades on factor shares.[21] Using the coefficient from the capital-labor ratio in this regression to extract the effects of labor-intensive competition, he then calculates the price changes that such competition entails. Finally he multiplies these price changes (possibly scaled up or down to reflect the presumed degree of competition) by Stolper-Samuelson elasticities that he has inferred from a regression of outputs on factor endowments, and this gives him his estimates of factor price changes. The results indicate a substantial decline in the unskilled wage due to the NAFTA.

This is a clever method of answering a very difficult question. As in the case of the Lawrence and Slaughter analysis, we are concerned that it relies heavily on the strong mathematical properties of the H-O model. In particular, it seems to require equal numbers of goods and factors in order for the Stolper-Samuelson elasticities to be well defined. It also does not allow for the kinds of economies of scale and competition effects that are often thought to be important in determining the effects of free trade in small countries.[22] And perhaps more seriously, we find it hard to accept the assumption that competition with Mexico will be qualitatively the same as the increased competition of the past few decades. Leamer's own discussion of Mexico as a "platform" for exports to the United States—which plays no role in his empirical analysis—seems to suggest that Mexico's role in a free trade agreement (FTA) will be different from the competition that we have experienced before.

---

21. Actually, he used data from only 1972–1985 for this regression, a period during which labor's share fell by a few percentage points. Over a longer period, 1950–1990, labor's share has remained essentially unchanged. We do not know how Leamer's choice of period may have affected his results.

22. See Brown, Deardorff, and Stern (1993), which discusses how these considerations can alter the relationship between prices and wages in an otherwise Stolper-Samuelson framework. Brown, Deardorff, and Stern (1992) reports increases in real wages for all three NAFTA countries, largely because of scale economies.

Conclusion

We set out to provide a selective survey of the empirical literature on trade and wages, and we chose to structure our discussion around the questions that this literature was asking. We found a good deal of interesting and important work, with some useful and informative results. To facilitate comparison, we have summarized the results of some of the studies that look at the effects of international trade on *relative* wages in table 3–1.[23] From this table it is clear that the studies do not reach a unified conclusion. Moreover, the studies do not even address many of the questions we initially set out.

Does protection affect wages? Only Gaston and Trefler (1992) and Leamer (1992) even try to answer that question, and their answers are hardly conclusive. Yet the question is in the consciousness of the public at large, which seems to have little doubt as to the answer. Trade theorists may think they know the answer, based on the Stolper-Samuelson theorem, but we still have little empirical evidence to back it up.

Does variation in trade permit events abroad to change wages at home? That question is also high in the minds of the public, concerning as it does the vulnerability of the U.S. labor force to "international competition." Yet none of the studies we looked at attempt empirically to isolate foreign from domestic reasons for quantities or prices of trade to change, and therefore they do not address this question.[24]

---

23. Our interpretation of the questions that are being addressed in all of the studies mentioned in table 3–1 is that they are of the more general "but for" form: But for any changes in trade volumes/prices, and regardless of the reasons for these changes, how would wages have behaved differently than they in fact did?

24. Johnson and Stafford (1992, 1993) have elaborated a theoretical argument that technical progress abroad, particularly in the newly industrializing countries, may have been a source of decline in wages in the United States and other industrialized countries. The reasoning is that, as these countries have acquired the technologies that were previously exclusive to the industrialized countries, the latter have suffered a worsening of their terms of trade. If this argument were verified empirically, it would suggest a loss to the industrialized countries due to a change abroad (technical progress) that was transmitted internationally through trade. That would not mean there had been a loss from trade per se, however, since what was lost would only be a portion of the earlier, larger gains from trade. The decline over time could have been avoided by not trading, but only by pushing welfare to the much lower autarky level early on and leaving it there.

We have not included the Johnson-Stafford work in our survey here because it is not empirical.

TABLE 3–1

EXTENT TO WHICH CHANGES IN RELATIVE WAGES CAN BE ACCOUNTED FOR
BY INTERNATIONAL TRADE, ACCORDING TO THE STUDIES SURVEYED,
1991–1993

Study	Effect of Trade	Detailed Explanation
Borjas, Freeman, and Katz (1991)	Substantial	Trade and immigration flows caused between 30–50% of the 10% decline in the relative weekly wage of high school dropouts, 1980–1988 Trade deficit caused between 15–25% of the 11% rise in the earnings of college graduates relative to high school graduates, 1980–1985
Murphy and Welch (1991)	Substantial	Exact match exists between the signs of relative labor demand changes predicted by changes in international trade with both the observed changes in the distribution of employment between industries and relative wages
Katz and Murphy (1992)	Some effect	Trade-induced changes in relative demand move in the correct direction to explain wage differentials, but are quite small in magnitude
Bound and Johnson (1992)	Little or none	Effects of trade are negligible, because estimates of total relative demand shifts are small
Leamer (1992)	Substantial	Estimates changes in real earnings induced by low-wage foreign competition to range from a $3,038–$30,384 increase for professional or technical workers, an increase of $7–$67 for every $1,000 of capital, and a decline of $931–$9,312 for the earnings of other workers (calculated including petroleum refining)
Lawrence and Slaughter (1993)	None	Dismiss trade as an explanation for relative wage changes, since international prices move in the wrong direction from those expected by the Stolper-Samuelson theorem for the observed changes in relative wages

SOURCE: Authors.

The question most commonly addressed is the more general one, of whether variations in trade make a country's labor force more or less vulnerable to shocks of all sorts, whether foreign or domestic. And there the evidence is mixed.

For the first half of the 1980s, changes in trade were associated with disruption in U.S. labor markets. The U.S. trade deficit expanded dramatically and unevenly across sectors, indicative of strains on the associated labor markets that in turn may have depressed unskilled wages, especially as compared with skilled wages. It may also be true that some of these changes could have been avoided if policies had prevented the changes in trade from taking place. There is no indication, however, that the causes of these changes came from abroad, or that restraining trade would have been desirable. Most likely, the source of the changes was the stance of the U.S. macroeconomic policy of the period, which led to a substantial expansion of expenditure relative to income. Had trade deficits not been possible, this expansion might also not have been possible, but the role of trade in this accident of history was more that of bystander than of instigator.

Similarly, over the longer period that includes the 1970s, changes in trade were again accompanied by changes in real and relative wages. Because the studies do not always do a good job of distinguishing induced changes in trade from other underlying causes of changes in both trade and wages, it is not easy to identify with confidence the causes of these changes. Evidence suggests, though, that they resulted from changes in technology that have occurred at home and abroad. Several studies, approaching the problem from quite different directions—from Bound and Johnson (1992) to Lawrence and Slaughter (1993)—have reached this conclusion, and we are inclined to agree.

In the end, the literature on trade and wages has told us something interesting and important about technology and wages. In our view, however, it has not answered convincingly the question that may be most on the minds of the public: whether U.S. workers have suffered from increased competition, through trade, with workers abroad.

References

Bhagwati, Jagdish. "Protection, Real Wages, and Real Incomes." *Economic Journal,* December 1959.

———. "Free Traders and Free Immigrationists: Strangers or Friends?" Russell Sage Foundation Working Paper no. 20. New York, N.Y.: Russell Sage Foundation, April 1991[a].

———. "Trade and Income Distribution." Paper presented at the Columbia University conference on deindustrialization, New York, N.Y., November 15–16, 1991[b].

Bhagwati, Jagdish, and Vivek Dehejia. "Freer Trade and Wages of the Unskilled—Is Marx Striking Again?" Chapter 2 of this volume.

Borjas, George J., Richard B. Freeman, and Lawrence F. Katz. "On the Labor Market Effects of Immigration and Trade." National Bureau of Economic Research, Working Paper no. 3761, 1991.

Bound, John, and George Johnson. "Wages in the United States during the 1980s and Beyond." In Marvin H. Kosters, ed., *Workers and Their Wages: Changing Patterns in the United States*. Washington, D.C.: AEI Press, 1991.

———. "Changes in the Structure of Wages during the 1980s: An Evaluation of Alternative Explanations." *American Economic Review*, vol. 82, 1992, pp. 371–92.

Brown, Drusilla K. "The Impact of a North American Free Trade Agreement: Applied General Equilibrium Models." In Nora Lustig, Barry Bosworth, and Robert Lawrence, eds., *North American Free Trade: Assessing the Impact*. Washington, D.C.: The Brookings Institution, 1992.

Brown, Drusilla K., Alan V. Deardorff, and Robert M. Stern. "A North American Free Trade Agreement: Analytical Issues and a Computational Assessment." *The World Economy*, January 1992, pp. 11–29.

———. "Protection and Real Wages: Old and New Trade Theory and Their Empirical Counterparts." Forthcoming work [1993].

Davis, Steven J. "Cross-Country Patterns of Change in Relative Wages." In Olivier J. Blanchard and Stanley Fischer, eds., *1992 Macroeconomic Annual*. Cambridge, Mass.: MIT Press, 1992.

Deardorff, Alan V. "FIRless FIRwoes: How Preferences Can Interfere with the Theorems of International Trade." *Journal of International Economics*, vol. 20, February 1986, pp. 131–42.

———. "Trade Policy of the Reagan Years." In Anandi P. Sahu and Ronald L. Tracy, eds., *The Economic Legacy of the Reagan Years: Euphoria or Chaos?* New York: Praeger Publishers, 1991, pp. 187–203.

———. "Overview of the Stolper-Samuelson Theorem." In Alan V. Deardorff and Robert M. Stern, eds., *The Stolper-Samuelson Theorem: A Golden Jubilee*. Ann Arbor, Mich.: University of Michigan Press. Forthcoming work [1993].

Deardorff, Alan V., and Jon Haveman. "Effect of U.S. Trade Laws on Poverty in America." Forthcoming work [1993].

Deardorff, Alan V. and Robert W. Staiger. "An Interpretation of the Factor Content of Trade." *Journal of International Economics*, vol. 24, February 1988, pp. 93–107.

Freeman, Richard B., and Lawrence F. Katz. "Industrial Wage and Employment Determination in an Open Economy." In John M. Abowd and Richard B. Freeman, eds., *Immigration, Trade, and the Labor Market*. Chicago: University of Chicago Press, 1991.

Gaston, Noel, and Daniel Trefler. "Protection, Trade, and Wages: Evidence for U.S. Manufacturing." Unpublished paper, 1992.

Grossman, Gene M. "Imports as a Cause of Injury: The Case of the U.S. Steel Industry." *Journal of International Economics*, vol. 20, 1986, pp. 201–23.

————. "The Employment and Wage Effects of Import Competition in the United States." *Journal of International Economic Integration*, vol. 2, 1987, pp. 1–23.

Johnson, George E., and Frank Stafford. "Models of Real Wages and International Competition." Discussion Paper no. 314, Research Forum on International Economics, Institute of Public Policy Studies/Department of Economics, University of Michigan, 1992.

————. "International Competition and Real Wages." *American Economic Review*, May 1993.

Jones, Ronald W. "The Structure of Simple General Equilibrium Models." *Journal of Political Economy*, December 1965, pp. 557–72.

————. "A Three-Factor Model in Theory, Trade, and History." In J. N. Bhagwati, R. W. Jones, R. A. Mundell, and J. Vanek, eds., *Trade, Balance of Payments, and Growth: Essays in Honor of Charles P. Kindleberger*. Amsterdam: North-Holland, 1971.

Katz, Lawrence, and Kevin M. Murphy. "Changes in Relative Wages, 1963–1987: Supply and Demand Factors." *Quarterly Journal of Economics*, vol. 107, 1992, pp. 35–78.

Katz, Lawrence, and Ana Revenga. "Changes in the Structure of Wages: The United States vs. Japan." *Journal of the Japanese and International Economies*, vol. 3, 1989, pp. 522–23.

Kosters, Marvin H. "An Overview of Changing Wage Patterns in the Labor Market." Chapter 1 of this volume.

Lawrence, Robert Z., and Matthew J. Slaughter. "Trade and U.S. Wages: Great Sucking Sound or Small Hiccup?" Faculty Research Working Paper Series, John F. Kennedy School of Government, Harvard University, 1993.

Leamer, Edward E. "Wage Effects of a U.S.–Mexican Free Trade Agreement." National Bureau of Economic Research Working Paper no. 3991. Cambridge, Mass.: NBER, 1992.

Mayer, Wolfgang. "Short-Run and Long-Run Equilibrium for a Small Open Economy." *Journal of Political Economy*, vol. 82, 1974, pp. 955–67.

Murphy, Kevin M., and Finis Welch. "The Role of International Trade in Wage Differentials." In Marvin H. Kosters, ed., *Workers and Their*

Wages: Changing Patterns in the United States. Washington, D.C.: AEI Press, 1991.

———. "The Structure of Wages." *Quarterly Journal of Economics,* vol. 107, 1992, pp. 285–326.

Mussa, Michael. "Tariffs and the Distribution of Income: The Importance of Factor Specificity, Substitutability, and Intensity in the Short and Long Run." *Journal of Political Economy,* vol. 82, 1974, pp. 1191–1204.

Revenga, Ana L. "Exporting Jobs: The Impact of Import Competition on Employment and Wages in U.S. Manufacturing." *Quarterly Journal of Economics,* vol. 107, 1992, pp. 255–84.

Samuelson, Paul A. "Ohlin Was Right." *Swedish Journal of Economics,* vol. 73, 1971, pp. 365–84.

Srinivasan, T. N., and John Whalley. *General Equilibrium Trade Policy Modeling.* Cambridge, Mass.: MIT Press, 1986.

A NOTE ON THE BOOK

This book was edited by
Cheryl Weissman
of the staff of the AEI Press.
The text was set in Palatino, a typeface designed by
the twentieth-century Swiss designer Hermann Zapf.
Coghill Composition, of Richmond, Virginia,
set the type, and Data Reproductions Corporation,
of Rochester Hills, Michigan, printed and bound the book,
using permanent acid-free paper.

The AEI PRESS is the publisher for the American Enterprise Institute for
Public Policy Research, 1150 17th Street, N.W., Washington, D.C. 20036;
Christopher C. DeMuth, publisher; *Dana Lane*, director; *Ann Petty*, editor; *Cheryl
Weissman*, editor; *Lisa Roman*, editorial assistant (rights and permissions).